I Have Been Assigned the Single Bird

I HAVE BEEN ASSIGNED THE SINGLE BIRD

A Daughter's Memoir

Susan Cerulean

The University of Georgia Press *Athens*

A Wormsloe
FOUNDATION
nature book

Some personal and place names have been changed
throughout the book to protect the privacy of the
individuals and institutions involved in this story.

Image on page iii: Adobe Stock | Leonard
Images on pages vi, 8, and 65: David Moynahan

Designed by Erin Kirk
Set in 10.5/15 Fournier
Printed and bound by Sheridan Books
The paper in this book meets the guidelines for
permanence and durability of the Committee on
Production Guidelines for Book Longevity of the
Council on Library Resources.

Most University of Georgia Press titles are
available from popular e-book vendors.

Printed in the United States of America
24 23 22 21 20 C 5 4 3 2 1

Library of Congress Number: 2020003819
ISBN: 9780820357379 (hardback : alk. paper)
ISBN: 9780820357386 (ebook)

For Jeff, life companion

and

For Bobbie, Irish twin

Contents

I Have Been Assigned the Single Bird

Looking after shorebird nests on an island in Apalachicola Bay.
Photo by the author.

Prologue

Our bodies return our bones to the Earth in many ways. For some, strokes and hemorrhages ricochet like a sort of internal lightning inside the brain or through the heart and arteries. Such was my father's fate, and for him, those strokes led to dementia and a long decline. It fell to me and my husband, Jeff, to care for that sweet man during the last five years of his life. As many people do, we struggled to reconcile the minutia of the bedside with our full-time work, with three sons to raise, and with the urgent call to speak and act on behalf of our climate and the besieged wildlife of Florida.

The writer William Kittredge once said: "I dream of the single-hearted heaven that is the coherent self."

In the face of dementia, a coherent life for any of us seemed out of the question. Jeff and I knew that if we took my dad into our home, the chaos dismantling his brain and body would overwhelm us. So we rented a room in an assisted living facility only a mile away, and there we saw to his care.

One afternoon, during the second September of my father's stay in the nursing home, I stood near his bed and pressed my forehead against the window. Through the glass, I could hear the muffled calls of cardinals and red-eyed vireos. I did not open the windows, for the late summer air steamed like a thick hot pudding.

When we first moved Dad into that room, the emerald light filtering through the windows had reminded me of swimming underwater in a warm river. It wasn't really so bad, like you might fear kudzu-mediated sunlight could be. But as time passed, I noticed that many of the tall pines around the nursing home were dying under the weight of the vines swarming their living canopies. I saw that those smothering lianas were like the tangles and plaques in my father's brain, how both kudzu and Alzheimer's replace a vibrant living place—a brain once full of inborn competence and memories of long-gone houses and long-grown children—dissolve those things in super-slow motion, replacing them with loss. Dad's drugs, the Namenda and the Aricept, were like winter frost in the forest. For a time, they would keep the plaques in his brain at bay. Link by link, the invasive vines weighted that scaffold of mature trees with blankets of biomass. I could still make out the biggest magnolia setting its red fall fruit, but I didn't know if it would survive until freezing December nights slashed the tough kudzu back to its knees.

During the time we cared for my father, I began to volunteer as a steward of wild shorebirds on several islands along the north Florida coast.

Two or three times a month between March and August, I'd slide my kayak down the concrete ramp at Ten Foot Hole in Apalachicola.

I'd tidy my lines, floating in the backwater basin between a double row of houseboats, sailboats, party boats, deep-sea fishing boats. I came to know them like I did each home on my own street in town. Some of the sailors and anglers recognized me too. I liked to imagine I was becoming part of the place, the background, not on a first-name basis, but worth a nod, not a startle. The fisher folk might not have known where I was going or what my job was, but I felt as if I were a moving piece of the working waterfront. Not a tourist.

My territory was a tiny island just south of the Apalachicola bridge where I was to locate and keep track of any birds nesting on the small, tear-drop-shaped island: most likely candidates were least terns, black skimmers, certain small plovers, or American oystercatchers.

I'd line up the prow of my boat with the red channel markers and adjust to the tide and the river's wide current. Then I'd push my shoulders into my double-bladed paddle and align with a mindset that might make me as much a part of the scenery on my upcoming bird survey as I was among the people of the boat ramp. That was my goal. Otherwise, as I entered the birds' nesting ground, I would be perceived as a threat. I imagined fading into quiet, becoming background, being benign. *I am a simple being, only passing through. I have a familiar aspect and trajectory. Don't be afraid, not of me.* I cloaked myself in that mantra.

Very quickly I found a single oystercatcher brooding her eggs on the sand. Over her long orange dagger of a bill, through scarlet-rimmed eyes, she had been tracking my approach long before I saw her. Her eye saw my paddle slicing the quiet waters of the boat ramp, watched my path unfolding, even before I myself had ascertained the mood of the wind. Never should I think that my eyes are brighter and more alert than hers, she who has sifted into this landscape every day of her life, and every day of the lives of her kind, for millions of years. From that long perspective, she watched me from her nest scrape on the sand. Three eggs burned into her belly through her brood patch. Her job was to watch for danger.

Was I danger, was I really?

Need her pulse sharpen, need she spring off the nest and expose her eggs to the sun in order to draw my eye off the little shingle of beach that was home for her shell-bound brood?

Correct. Yes. Absolutely.

Yes. Our human selves are a grave danger to everything wild and vulnerable on the planet.

I didn't know the Earth was afflicted by our species until I was well into my twenties. All I wanted to do was submerge myself in the delight of it, and I did: the Atlantic Ocean, cold and dark and irresistible. Piles of autumn leaves: scarlet, orange, cadmium yellow. Canoe expeditions through the pitcher plant bogs of the Okefenokee Swamp and the chill of the Suwannee River's springs. I took those wild places and the reliable turn of the seasons for granted. Excesses of winter simply meant a pair of snow days; summer, a brief wave of heat. There was no reason to imagine the seasons would ever lose the structure they offered my life. The natural world was mine to dwell on, and I did.

But now I understand that all of the ways that our coast and its islands, our springs and our native birds, and our panthers and our Everglades are being diminished are symptoms of our culture's commitment to infinite growth. Infinite taking isn't possible on a finite planet. The sky, for example, is not a vast and limitless expanse. As Al Gore has said, our atmosphere is a shockingly thin envelope. We are changing its chemical composition by emitting 110 million tons of man-made global warming pollutants into our delicate atmosphere every day, as if it were an open sewer. These actions are both unethical and rife with repercussions, not just for future generations of humans but for all species with whom we share the Earth.

In the 1950s and 1960s, when I was a child, we knew so little about chronic diseases of the mind, body, and spirit, and what we did know, we kept to ourselves. Cancer was the big C, depression had no name at all, and the word *alcoholism* was never used. So when Alzheimer's came creeping into my father's brain, our family had had a lifetime's training in not naming—and not really knowing—what was going on, not just illness but also the shame that comes with it, and the helpless, hidden sorrow. We couldn't have named, at that time, its emotional potency.

So let's say it out loud: dementia. The word *dementia* comes from the Latin *demens*, meaning madness, or the irreversible deterioration of the intellectual properties of the brain.

De (undoing) plus *mens* (the mind). That's dementia.

Alzheimer's, Pick's, Lewy body, Parkinson's: these are not the natural result of aging but are specific, identifiable diseases of the brain. Most dementing illnesses do their damage gradually. Then, as they progress, the affected person loses intellect, abstract thinking, judgment, and memory and eventually descends into complete disorder and oblivion.

The Earth is the brain and the body into which we were born. In some nearly parallel way, we face not only a crisis in numbers of people diagnosed with dementia; as a culture, we are stricken with this disease and its attending violence. Why else would we knowingly destroy the planet that sustains our very lives? Our Western economic and political systems, all the ways we personally consume and give over our power to corporations and oligarchs—those are the illnesses that are killing our planet. When you have the physical disease, you experience it alone. But our cultural dementia—we are in this together.

What is our part, what can each one of us do, to alter the trajectory we ride? How can we bring healing to this world? My deepest desire regarding both my father's illness and the Earth's biosphere and biodiversity was to save, to rescue, to ensure continuance, and for many years, I thought I could.

I learned this conviction from my father, who cultivated in his children an earnest commitment to repair the broken world, beginning with what ailed our own family. One Friday, a teacher-planning day (meaning our mother had to work in her classroom but we four kids were home from school), Dad prepared a ceremonial lunch to enlist our support. He set the maple dining room table with placemats and the brown, glazed soup bowls we rarely used. He served us lentil soup and good bread on a cutting board and a fragrant wedge of cheddar. Everything about that meal was unusual, especially our mom's empty chair.

"Kids, we need to do more to help your mother," he said, carefully slicing the cheese. We did not understand what weighed on her so heavily, nor did he; but we knew she was in a dark place. He hoped it would relieve her if we contributed more to the running of the household. To me and Bobbie, he assigned the family's laundry, and we agreed to try. Our mother's depression, fueled by alcohol, was not fixable with detergent and an ironing board, and certainly not by her children, but that wasn't something we could know yet. What my dad recognized was that something was deeply wrong in our home. Something was wrong with our mother. Now I understand that something is deeply wrong with our Mother Earth.

I offer you the story of my own explorations in service to this question: How can we care for this world? I have tried to reconcile my roles as one daughter caring for one father, as one woman attuned at times to only a single wild bird while the planet is burning. How I long to change the world for the better. Offering care to those we love is closely similar to standing up for our Earth. In all cases, we are required to be fierce and full-bodied advocates, in an endless series of small actions, each as important as the next. This story braids the human and the animal, as it must, for we can never be separate.

PART I

Plover

Beneath the currents
of birds
I see the bevel in the world

And carry it in the sluice
of bird wing

There was a scurry
in bird step
I sought to mimic

Maybe there is an urgency
to saving the doomed
folds of the creek,

Maybe I can breathe
the milk of passing
air

and fold beneath my
rising sky.

JAY SNODGRASS

CHAPTER I

Diagnosis

"Something is wrong, Sue." My father's face was a wrinkled up question.

I stepped past a sliding glass door onto the small garden patio. Two padded lounge chairs faced a tripod of empty bird feeders. A fragrant veil of smoke and spattering of meat brought a flash of comfort, reminding me of the many cookouts we'd shared when our family was young.

My sister Bobbie and I had converged at our father's house from our own homes in Connecticut and Florida. In the kitchen, Bobbie sliced summer tomatoes and sweet onions. "I'll go keep him company," I had said to her.

But Dad was bent oddly over the flames. A pair of tongs and a spatula extended his reach like the right and left claws of a blue crab. I moved to his side.

He had lit squares of charcoal, which glowed in a tidy heap on the bottom of the grill. All good. But my father had laid the raw hamburger patties directly on the coals. He had forgotten to use the rack that suspended the meat above the flames, and he could not puzzle out what had gone wrong. He clacked unfruitfully at the meat with his implements.

I stood at the grill beside my dad, caught between nervous laughter (*could this be a joke?*) and horror.

Something is wrong, Sue.

On that day, my sister and I began to square with our new reality.

It wasn't just the one incident. Weeks earlier, as I stood in my own kitchen in Florida rinsing garden lettuce for a salad, the telephone jangled. I reached across the stove for the phone, timing in my head the enchiladas baking in the oven. Bits of middle school band melody drifted from the bedrooms of my sons. An ordinary moment. And then it was not.

"Your dad has had a stroke," said my stepmother, Mary Jane. Her voice shook over the telephone I pressed hard against my ear. "A small one. Yesterday. We didn't know what happened at first. Out of the blue, he couldn't say anything that made sense, except for one word: *store*."

I stayed quiet on my end of the line, drying my free hand on a dishtowel, absorbing her words.

"Store," she said. "That was the only word he could say. He just kept repeating *store*."

Mary Jane told me she couldn't figure out what Dad was trying to communicate, didn't know what she should do. So, she told me, she drove Dad to a quickie mart and they bought a six-pack of beer.

What could I say to that?

"This morning your dad's speech hadn't improved, so I took him to the hospital," she continued. "The emergency room doctor told us your dad had had a ministroke and sent us home to rest."

Dad had a stroke and they drove to the store for beer. Never had the nine hundred miles between Florida and New Jersey stretched so far.

I had been content to be a daughter from the distance of my north Florida home, traveling to New Jersey as often as I could, alternating visits with my three siblings. My husband, Jeff, and I had full-time jobs, and two young teenagers still to raise. And Dad was comfortably settled with his new wife, Mary Jane, the last of his five wives.

My father hated to be alone. He was generous and quick to love and wanted to share all of his heart, all of the time. He had remarried only eight months after my mother died in 1975, and then three times again over the next twenty years. Two of those wives—the second and the third—had been hasty, short-lived picks. The last two were gems, including Mary Jane.

But our weekly phone conversations had become centered around Mary Jane's frustrations. Our stepmother hadn't signed on for Dad's dementia. No one ever does. And everything got harder.

"Your father has lost his keys again," she'd say. And "He can't add up his checkbook anymore." And "He won't go anywhere without me." Impatience crackled like heat lightning in her voice. Yet no one thing seemed like a terribly big deal to me. My grandparents had aged and died without requiring much help, and if I thought about it at all, I assumed that would be true of my dad.

"You can't believe how awful it was," said my sister, over the phone. She had driven Dad and Mary Jane to hear the neurologist's diagnosis: Alzheimer's disease.

"I think the worst of it for Dad was the threat to take away his car keys." Bobbie called Dad's church to rally support. The minister had already realized something wasn't right.

"He says Dad comes in every couple days and stands in the office. Same thing at the doctor's office. He just shows up at the receptionist's desk. He doesn't even go so far as to ask: *Please, can you help me?*" Bobbie reported the facts, but her voice choked. "Breaks my heart. Poor old guy."

I imagined our father steering his gray SUV into those parking lots, screwing up his courage, probably guessing that neither minister nor doctor had a solution for the disease that was invading his brain. In the late 1990s, dementia bore a stigma that shuttered meaningful conversation. But he went there anyway, going where he had always gone, trusting the institutions he'd always trusted to put things right.

A few days after his diagnosis, I phoned my father and asked what it felt like to be in his body. "I feel like the world is spinning out of control," he said. We both knew the short-term losses to come: his car, his independence. He'd always been a man on the move.

"Goofy," he said. "I feel odd. It's almost funny that I can't say with my voice what I have in my head."

"My brother sent me an article from *Newsweek* about the brain, about Alzheimer's disease," Dad said. He went on to tell me how plaque builds up in the arteries of the brain. It was more of a conversation—and an acknowledgment—than we'd had about Dad's illness so far.

I said, "Actually, Dad, your voice does sound a little peculiar." I was wondering if his tongue was thickening. I had been reading about Alzheimer's symptoms too. A good friend had recommended a caregiver's guide that laid out the progression of the illness in stages. Back then, in the beginning, I thought this was a disease with a timeline, that we could pace ourselves.

"Oh, that's just because I am lying down on the couch while I am talking to you. I feel kind of sick to my stomach."

Both he and Mary Jane suspected a doubled ration of his new Alzheimer's pills was the cause, but Dad didn't want to cut back the dosage. He was frightened he would lose whatever benefit against the dementia they might provide.

Despite growing up alongside my mother's chronic illness—was it depression or alcoholism, or the latter an attempt to medicate the first—still I'd emerged into young adulthood with a remarkably optimistic belief in saving things. I thought we could save the world, or my adopted state of Florida, at least. I'd been hired as a wildlife biologist in 1984 as part of the state wildlife agency's new Nongame Wildlife Program. It was a heady time for an energetic person who wanted to advocate for wildlife. There were many of us, and we were encouraged in our work, never attacked. We believed in good science and a stewardship ethic, and our chain of command did not hold us back or muzzle us. Governor Bob Graham listened intently to the great conservation leaders of the time, and in successive sessions, the Florida legislature (Democrats and Republicans working together!) not only funded the Nongame Wildlife Program but established water-quality standards, addressed wetlands protection, required local governments to start planning how to handle Florida's explosive growth, and set in motion what for many years was the nation's most successful land-acquisition program.

Diagnosis of Florida's ills seemed simple. Identify the trends. Take them one at a time, figure out what's causing the problem. Repair what's wrong.

Take the Florida black bear. In the 1980s, black bears, though classified as a threatened species, were still hunted in Florida. It was rare back then to see one. You could ride along Highway 319 from the Ochlockonee River bridge to the FSU Marine Lab and maybe one year, maybe twenty years after you started hoping and watching, you'd spot something larger than a dog, with longer legs than you could believe. It would lope across the highway in front of your car and you would turn to your companions and try to find words to describe the thrilling quality of the animal, like no bear you'd ever seen sleeping at the Tallahassee Junior Museum or in a zoo. Most of all you'd notice the athletic stretch of its limbs, so clearly built for pacing the many square miles of its huge home range.

Once in a while, I would attend meetings of the agency's appointed commissioners, and I felt both frightened and fascinated by the bear hunters who came to advocate for their sport. They didn't suit up like the staff bureaucrats or the wealthy

Florida black bears bounced back after a ban on sport hunting in 1994.
Photo by David Moynahan.

landowners and corporate businessmen on the commission. They wore camou-
flage pants, leather boots, and caps pulled low over their eyes. I saw more than
one scratch his spine against a post, as if he were a bear and the post a tree. If you
squinted your eyes, you could imagine the hunters as forest animals. They seemed
of an earlier time in Florida, when this land was an open frontier and everything—
land and wildlife alike—was up for trapping or shooting, skinning or eating. I
simply couldn't believe that anyone wanted to shoot a bear for sport. And yet, they
did. And I also knew that those hunters and I shared the same love of wild woods.

In 1994, bear hunting was closed statewide: science, and perhaps reason, or even
morality, prevailed. The bear hunters were forced back into their forest camps and
inholdings and to silence their guns. Bears began to bounce back.

So saving wild things seemed concretely doable, if not easy, at least if the problem was hunting a threatened species for sport. I'd yet to learn that there was so
much more we'd have to address, beyond stopping the shooting. The deaths of

birds and other wild animals I'd witnessed were usually single and after the fact. A cardinal killed after crashing against a window. Hawks and owls reduced to feathered mop heads on the side of the road. Once, a snowy egret shot then roasted over a bonfire by some children in Perry, Florida. I'd yet to face the underlying causes of my state's diminishing wildlife: rampant overdevelopment and habitat loss.

CHAPTER 2

Hot Metal, and a Medal

From a lounge chair on her patio, my stepmother, Mary Jane, reached up her arms to greet me. She wore a sleeveless pink shell and plaid shorts, and her legs, freckled brown, were stretched in the sun. The bones in her shoulders felt like little bird wings—tiny wings, fragile wings—when we embraced.

"Your father is upstairs in his office," my stepmother said. "He will be so glad you are here." Before I turned to find my dad, I lingered a minute more with Mary Jane. In her elfin face, I could see my whole remembered past, though my mother had died decades before. She had been my mother's best friend from the time our families moved into newly constructed homes, side by side, in a north Jersey subdivision. Her five children and our four—two boys, seven girls—played together every summer day.

Two years had passed since my dad's diagnosis. Every six weeks, I flew to Philadelphia, where I'd rent a car and drive through the Jersey pine barrens to Dad and Mary Jane's home in Manahawkin. My sister Bobbie did the same, traveling south from her home in Connecticut. Between us, we felt like our parents were reasonably attended.

I pushed through the glass storm door and bounded up the steep carpeted stairs to my father's study. Dad half-rose from the couch to hug me, his face smiling and transparent with love. He wasn't a large man. He'd kept his hair—untouched by gray—and would until he died.

He didn't ask how my flight was or if I wanted a glass of tea.

"I'm sorting papers," my father said. "Seems like all I ever do is try to get myself organized." I settled close beside him on a small wicker chair.

Dad fidgeted through a binder of financial reports on his lap. "I've been wanting to show you this," he said. "Because I can't call you on the phone anymore." He didn't meet my eyes. "I guess the Alzheimer's disease makes it too hard to figure out . . ."

"The numbers on the dial?" I filled in his words.

Yes, he nodded, that was it. His forefinger traveled to the last number in the final column on the last page.

"This is what I've got set aside to leave to you kids," he said. "Do you think it's enough?"

"I feel sure it is, Dad," I said, studying the numbers at the bottom of the page. Anything he left us would be a gift. My own worry was different than his: what would be the course of this disease, and how would our family see to his care?

I was glad my father didn't ask about my job, for I was restless. The Nongame Wildlife Program had blossomed and become absorbed into the larger agency, now employing more than thirty biologists and educators. For me it had been a place to be creative, to conjure new programs that might teach and motivate our state's populace to protect wildlife. We wrote a guidebook to viewing wildlife in Florida and developed a Watchable Wildlife initiative to encourage counties to value their wildlands and creatures, if only for the economic benefits that might accrue. But I wanted to go deeper. I had cut my hours at the agency and traveled to Montana and Colorado to study with Terry Tempest Williams and Linda Hogan, exploring new ways to write and speak about the animals I knew were declining and about the ways of our colonizing culture. I intensely wanted to know how my people fit into this bigger, tougher picture. I thought if I understood, then I'd know my role. My book *Tracking Desire: A Journey after Swallow-tailed Kites* was published, and I'd sent ahead a signed copy to my parents before this visit.

After dinner, Mary Jane shooed us off into the living room to visit while she cleaned up the dishes. Dad picked up my book from the coffee table. I perched on a hassock near his armchair, wondering what he would think about my book's more personal aspects.

"I think your book is wonderful, the best writing you've ever done," Dad said, creasing open the cover to the table of contents. He traced his fingers over the chapter titles, crossed his legs at the knee. Then he closed the book and folded his hands in his lap. He met my eyes, a long look for him, his eyes so unprotected, so vulnerable, liquid gray.

"What specifically did you like, Dad?"

My mother (right) would have approved: decades after her death,
Dad married her close friend Mary Jane Grambor.

"All the adjectives," he said. We couldn't leave it at that.

And then the things I feared—knew—would sting him tumbled out between us.

"You hated the company I worked for, didn't you?" Dad said. "And it was awful to make you move when Inco transferred me when you all were so young."

"Oh, please don't feel hurt, Dad," I said, placing my hand over his cool fingers. "I was just trying to write my own version of how life has formed me. You have been the best father ever." I knew the truth of his goodness. My father meant no harm, not ever. Moreover, it was he who had taught me to care about the world and gifted me with the books of Rachel Carson as one by one they were published. It was my dad who had taught me to caress the muscly trunk of the ironwood tree and the rough mittens of the sassafras shrub and commit to memory their places in the mountain forest near our home. And it was Dad who had brought home a new, mint-green clothbound *Peterson Field Guide to Birds* and held it at arm's length against the window, so we could learn the real birds outside. Every summer we'd begin all over again with Peterson and the shorebirds when we visited the shore, the skittering willets and sanderlings prodding the wet sand beach.

But now I felt driven to ferret out how my family's lifestyle was embedded in our country's extractive economy and to understand how we might be complicit.

I knew exactly the pages of my book that had hurt my father's heart. It was what I had pieced together about the company that had employed him—the International Nickel Company. Besides the need to support his family of six after World War II, Dad had a long enthusiasm for his chosen profession. "I loved working with hot metal," my father had told me of his early years of observing furnaces and smelters of steel. Later in life, when his work restricted him to offices and conference rooms, he volunteered as a blacksmith at a local state park.

But in my own research, I learned that those hot-red furnaces burned with ore ripped from the inner fastness of the Canadian landscape. Rivers ran metallic and poisonous downstream of those factories, and the air was vastly contaminated.

Dad was a very small cog in his company's resource-extraction machinery. His job was to market nickel ore to other industries, and so my family's comfortable middle-class standard of living was built on the mining of nonrenewable ores, so-called resources, from the body of the planet.

Nevertheless, as I sat with my father in the small pool of light in his living room that night, I saw that my attempt to understand was clumsy, and my framing of my father's life work was painful for him to read about in my book.

It wasn't just my words that stung him; it was the disease he knew was taking his mind. He rose from his chair and walked to the window facing the driveway where his car waited in the dark. "Pretty much breaks my heart," said Dad. Our father had just been banned by his doctor from driving this car, or any other, ever again. My brother was coming to retrieve it for his own son very soon.

"Sue, it's in perfect condition," said Dad, his voice choking to a whisper. "It's got seventy-one thousand miles on it, but there's not a thing wrong with it."

I thought of a black night four decades earlier, driving with my dad on a winding road in southern Michigan. Seatbelts with big buckles held us in place. Only the green and red lights on the dashboard illuminated the car's dim interior, and our headlamps revealed only the briefest stretch of the unrolling road. Trees leaned out of the pavement; we drove through a tunnel of branches and leaves. There were no other cars. I did not know where the road would take us. All I had to hang onto was my father, but I was too old to cling, physically or emotionally. I was thirteen, between sixth and seventh grades, and I'd be starting junior high school in this new town, leaving behind New Jersey and everything familiar. My dad had arranged that trip because he knew it would be hard for me to uproot. He was soft inside and he didn't want me to hurt. He imagined that if he showed me my new school with its big indoor pool, and singing classes, and cooking and sewing instruction, and five foreign languages, that I would be able to bear our family's relocation. He was defined by an instinct to care for us.

Most likely my dad didn't know exactly where he was going either. The large corporation he worked for had mandated his relocation and he had a wife and four children to support. Dad wasn't in a position to say no.

So there we were in the front seat of the car, driving through the dark unknown of our lives with all that space between us. Dad tried to cut it down to size by distracting me. He proposed a math puzzle.

"Okay, Susie, figure this one out. There are two trains leaving a city on parallel tracks, traveling the same direction. The passenger train is going twice as fast as the freight train. After forty-five minutes, the trains are thirty miles apart. What is the speed of each train?" He threw a quick glance at me in the passenger seat.

In my mind's eye, I saw this: How scary it would be (kind of like right now, traveling toward an unknown life) if I were on a train going a certain speed. Maybe I'd walk from train car to train car through the little rattling open spaces between the cars, where you could really feel the swinging of the train and the cold wind, when another train hurtled past with all those flashing lighted windows and the squealing brakes on steel tracks.

I knew that was what it was all about, why we were sent to Michigan. It had to do with steel and stainless steel and alloys of steel and most especially nickel. It was my father's employer, International Nickel, that severed our family from our roots and sent us to live in the Midwest. We knew nothing of what my dad had seen in the mines, nor the fiercely heated factories, nor for that matter, the war he'd fought. We knew he loved hot metal because he said so. Not because we'd ever seen any in our home or town. Although perhaps the train on the track was something like the foundries that generated that steel, forcing our culture into an ever-faster, more extractive future. My teacher Deena Metzger once said: "I want to tell you that a person can be wonderfully good, generous, kind, and still operate within the cultural machinery that destroys the Earth."

The struggle that had made my dad into a purposeful man was World War II.

"Sue, go back into my bedroom and fetch the little gold box on my nightstand," he said.

Inside the box, nestled in cotton, was a wafer-thin turquoise enamel medal engraved with an image of the Virgin Mary, also known as Our Lady of Lourdes. I held the exquisite icon close to the lamp between us. My throat ached with tears. I knew he'd gone to the jewelry store downtown to buy the fine silver chain holding the medal and used up one of his few chits for transport to do so. Mary Jane preferred to drive as little as possible, and Dad wasn't allowed behind the wheel.

"What a precious gift, Dad," I said, lifting my hair and fastening the silver clasp at the back of my neck. I knew the story of where this medal had come from, but I asked him to tell me again, to prolong the moment and the gift.

"Write it down so you remember," he said. I pulled a notebook and a pen from my backpack on the floor. Dad's eyes drifted out the window as he thought.

"It was a grand day, Sue," he said. "I'll never forget how the townspeople surrounded us as we entered Saint-Brieuc."

I pictured him in my mind: the youngest in his regiment of engineers, the slightest built, underage, but probably the most enthusiastic, marching into that small village in northwestern France, liberating it from the German occupation on August 6, 1944.

"Write that down," he emphasized, watching my pen move across the page. "We liberated the town! And all the people surrounded us and cheered. They were so very glad to see us! I can still see the face of the Frenchwoman who pressed this little medal into my hands."

That was the one constant point of pride in my dad's life, the time he spent as a very young man in the army. Before dementia had a name and a power over him, a gathering power, like a war, an ominous war against his brain and his body, Dad had been piecing together a personal memoir. When my sister and I saw it for the very first time a year earlier, the fact that three-quarters of the laboriously typed manuscript focused on his three years in World War II astonished us. He'd never talked much about the war when we were children.

Bobbie was plain mad. "What about us?" she had said. "Why didn't he write anything about his family?"

"It's not because we didn't count," I had tried to reassure her.

In bed that night, I snuggled deep under a navy comforter. A small replica of the Barnegat Lighthouse lit the darkened room. I thought about Dad, trapped in his slowed-down body, with a life and a car and an office he could no longer fully occupy. I could almost imagine how he might have felt in 1944.

Our yard was green, so green, and our lives so predictable. The narrow pine staircase that I climbed to my upstairs bedroom had begun to feel like a ladder to a jail cell. I was done with cleaning the chicken coop, drying dishes, maneuvering my mother's endless list of chores!

I had a longing I couldn't quell; it kept dropping lower and lower in my belly. In high school, I had fed it well enough, skating on snowy nights holding Sally Arnold's hand, or camping in a big khaki tent at Yaw Paw. The freedom of those things was enough.

But war was coming around again, and we knew it. We heard it on the radio; we read about it every day in the papers. And this called up inside me a purpose larger than I'd ever known in my life. It was like building a watchfire, something fine and bright, that's how I came to think of fighting overseas for our country. The brass notes of military music drifting in from our little town square poured kerosene on that burning inside me. I knew I could help set the world right even though I'd never been chosen for first-string basketball or anything but far outfield on the spring baseball team.

At the age of seventeen, Dad had gone down to the recruiter's office by himself to sign up for the army. The man had sent him home twice because his parents would not grant their approval. They did not want their son to go to war.

"You certainly may not sign up for the army, Robert," my mother had said. "Charles, you take our son back down there and get him unenlisted. Robert, you are too young, you will do no such thing." She drew her lips into a straight line. She would not grant me my life even though I wanted to be useful and I wanted to battle evil. Even though I was scared.

The third time my father tried to enlist in as many weeks, my grandmother and grandfather relented. The 1057th Engineers didn't serve on the front lines—their job was to rebuild bridges blown up by the retreating German armies—nevertheless, his journal and his letters home were laced with taut fear and repeated references to the "goings-on of the enemy."

The next day, Dad and I took over the kitchen to concoct his favorite German potato salad while Mary Jane went to the hairdresser. I laid strips of bacon in a frying pan. Potatoes bubbled on the stove. Our conversation was fragmentary, comfortable. But there was more I wanted to know about his past and mine, before he could no longer tell me.

"Dad, when you worked for Inco, did you ever visit the mines near Sudbury, in Ontario?" I asked.

My father raised his eyes from the fresh parsley he was chopping at the counter, startled. "How did you find out about that place?" he asked. Almost as if the mines were something he had pushed and hidden, way in the back of his mind. Or as if he felt I was prying, trying to understand how he made his living beyond what he was willing to tell (which in fact I was).

"Yes, I did," he said. I didn't tell him why I was inquiring, that I was intent on understanding my own family's investment in resource extraction that was destroying so much land and water and wildlife.

I stuck a fork into the potatoes and then poured them through a colander in the sink. Steam veiled my face and neck. At the table, Dad peeled three hard-boiled eggs, chopped them fine.

One by one, I lifted the crisped lengths of bacon onto a nest of paper towels to drain off the fat. Dad measured olive oil, vinegar, and spices for his special dressing into a small red bowl.

What a strange time we were in. My dad, who had supported me all my life, his memory beginning a long fade. Me, writing in defense of the natural world, as he had encouraged me to do, finding a mirror in human abuses and taking from the planet. I hadn't meant to make my father a scapegoat.

Unexpectedly, he began to talk about another long silence between us. He watched me slide the warm salad into the refrigerator. "You know, your mother tried to tell me several times what was going on with her."

My turn to startle. I had never heard him address that part of our family's past before. My mother's alcoholism and early death and whatever fueled those things—those were their secrets, or maybe just her secret—and our family's buried shame.

"What did she say, Dad?" It felt like my last chance to understand my mother, who had been dead more than twenty-seven years.

But he had no more words.

CHAPTER 3

Paths

Jeff and I set off at a half trot through a forest of Virginia pines, following a well-marked trail. The trees were wonderfully familiar in aspect to our southern pinewoods; the understory plants were not. No saw palmetto, no evergreens like gallberry or wax myrtle. But plenty of twiggy leafless shrubs with beautifully reddening new growth. Wild blueberries, I guessed.

"It's 2:06," said Jeff, looking at his watch. Our goal was to walk fast and make our hearts work. "How about we go for forty minutes?"

The day before, we'd flown up from Florida to be with Dad and Mary Jane. After all that hurtling through air and over asphalt, we had to will our bodies to slow down to match my parents' pace. It wasn't just my physical momentum that had to adjust. My mind was racing too. I wanted to fix their lives. And quickly.

"I have an idea about that thing we were talking about yesterday, about why it's hard for you to resolve your dad and Mary Jane's dilemma." Jeff spoke slowly, looking into my face. He didn't want to proceed without making sure I wouldn't bristle at his observations.

"Go ahead and tell me what you're thinking," I said. But he was right, inside my head, I was already defending myself.

"You know, as if they're children."

I tried to want to hear what he was going to say. "Give me an example," I said.

Jeff inspected my face again. A light sweat beaded his forehead. I knew he was tiptoeing around my pride, but I also knew he was a really good problem solver.

"Okay," he said. "I think sometimes you talk down to them. It may feel to them like we are trying to take over their decisions."

A little window opened in my mind. My response to my dad's illness was to try to find structure for his life and hers, to contain what was to come.

I thought back to breakfast.

"I do not want to move to assisted living," Mary Jane had said. *You have to*, I screamed silently. How else were they to get the help they needed?

But I couldn't come up with a single way to move the conversation forward. So how did I respond? I switched the topic to toast. "Why is this pumpernickel bread dark? Where does it get its color from?" I had said, spreading soft butter over a crusty heel.

None of the other three had an answer. I picked up the cellophane package and read the list of ingredients aloud. "Must be the caramel coloring," I said.

Why was I talking about pumpernickel bread? God, I wanted to go deep with them, but I could not for the life of me figure out how to get a meaningful conversation going—*in the direction I thought it should go.*

When Mary Jane wouldn't talk about hiring help around the house, or moving into assisted living, or at least closer to one of their children, I would back down, let the conversation die—and complain to my siblings later on. I couldn't say what I believed, which was that Dad had declined to a point where he would be lost without Mary Jane now. How could we help with his care from a thousand miles away? What would happen next?

Still, maybe Jeff was right. Maybe I was looking for a way to maneuver them to do what I thought was best. A part of me looked down at us jogging through the fragrant trees and saw the corners of my mouth curve up, just a little.

Later, in the car, Dad said: "I think I'll be dead by Christmas." Jeff and I exchanged glances, startled and curious. Mary Jane tightened her grip on the steering wheel, straightened her spine.

"Now, Bob," she scolded. "Remember what the doctor told us. You've got to stay optimistic. Alzheimer's doesn't kill people." Who was closing down the conversation now?

Alone with my father in his office, I asked him why he thought he'd soon be dead. "It's this disease," he said. He felt that dementia was—or would soon—kill his ability to be himself. I feared that too. Listlessness replaced the passion and curiosity that used to be the hallmark of my father. Dad seemed so tired. He slept long into the mornings, sometimes napped too, and was always the first to head for bed after dinner.

But he had things he wanted resolved, even if they weren't what worried me. "When I am gone, will someone write a loving summary of my life, as I did for my two dead wives?" he asked me.

"Of course we will!" I said.

"And have I told you what I want done with my ashes?" He didn't pause for my answer. "I want them flowing into the ocean halfway between Ocracoke and Hatteras Islands, just like we did with your mom's."

"I wonder how we will manage that," he added. He couldn't imagine not being there and taking care of things, even for his own funeral.

"Remember your eightieth birthday?" I asked. All four of us kids and many of his friends had prepared tributes and accolades, lengthy and heartfelt. He did, and he smiled, thinking back. Dad wasn't worried about his safety as much as we were. He just wanted to know he'd done his job and that we knew it too.

"Dinnertime!" Mary Jane called us to the table.

I stood behind Dad, waiting for him to inch down the carpeted stairs. His right hand gripped the smooth wooden rail. I could feel the effort of his intended locomotion. I rested my hand on his shoulder and inhaled the familiar scent of his wool vest and his shaving cream.

Back at home, my friend Norine and I shared a practice of walking together along the boardwalks and red clay roads out in the country, near the small town of Miccosukee, many times a week. We did it for the exercise, we did it to watch the moon rise and the wildflowers turn with the seasons, and we did it to clear our minds and reinforce our paths in the world, not just through these particular woods.

One afternoon, our trail took us over a boardwalk through a green-canopied swamp. The afternoon was heavy-clouded, low-ceilinged, on the lip of a gray front moving in from the west. Soon, the rain would come.

"Say we wanted to organize action on behalf of the Earth in a brand-new way," I proposed. "What would be our focus?"

"I think we've got to hold people more strictly accountable," Norine mused. She was a therapist and a passionate advocate, and we'd covered a lot of territory over the years. I held back an overhanging limb of swamp bay, allowing her to pass. A frog plopped into the blackwater creek.

"I think we need to ask ourselves—and others—to meaningfully pledge to act." She'd been studying the autobiography of Mahatma Gandhi, and she felt his tactics were a good way to organize.

"But act how?" I asked. "How can one person really help protect endangered species, when you've already got a full-time job and a family?" I had worked for the state wildlife agency and several conservation groups before that for nearly twenty years, and it was clear we were still losing ground.

Later that same evening, Jeff joined us for dinner on Norine's airy screened porch, and our conversation continued. I handed around white enamel bowls of black beans and rice.

"Here's the thing," said Jeff, an oceanographer and biogeochemist by training. He settled into a rocker and set a sweating bottle of beer on the porch rail. Far off in the swamp, a pair of barred owls began to call. "There's really only one issue that is driving all the rest and that's climate change."

I protested. "How could there be anything worse for wildlife than habitat loss?"

Jeff and his colleagues had understood that the climate was changing for some years, by now. But it wasn't reported much in the news, and to me, it was a new and unthinkably enormous concept. Bulldozers and asphalt trucks had seemed like more than enough to contend with.

Sitting together with my friend and my husband in the lowering evening, I began to really digest what none of us wanted to be true. That beginning in the eighteenth century, during the Industrial Revolution, as humans began to burn coal and gas and oil to produce energy and goods, the amount of carbon in the atmosphere started to accumulate, at first slowly and then ever more quickly. The product of our industrial respiration, millions of years' worth of carbon stored beneath the earth had been released, increasing in the atmosphere, and now it was spoiling our nest.

"What needs to be done is to teach people how our energy-happy culture is affecting all of life on Earth," Jeff said.

"I think stories are the best way for people to learn," said Norine.

Jeff thought for a while. "Okay, how about this? Imagine the deep ocean seafloor, a cold, dark place, barren of life. But every now and then a large bounty will arrive, let's say a dead whale drifts down from the surface. Then sea life explodes: all manner of worms and other invertebrates colonize the dead organic matter, and

Early harbingers of rising sea levels along Florida's Gulf Coast: dying cabbage palms.
Photo by David Moynahan.

their populations increase dramatically—for a short time. Inevitably the resource dwindles and the population collapses."

Through the screen, I watched lightning bugs hang their temporary lanterns in the darkening woods. A family of cardinals scudded into the trellised garden tomatoes.

"That's where we're headed," he said. "Humans fuel their economic growth in the same way. We've found our dead whale below ground, in the form of oil, gas, and coal—the fossil remains of plants that lived long ago."

I'd have to repurpose my path, my advocacy, if all this were really true, that wild birds and other animals weren't in decline simply because we crowded and shot them. We humans were affecting the very climate they had adapted to. The warming atmosphere was—or would become—our problem too.

But it wasn't an easy task, and it wasn't in my job description. I was developing maps and interpretive signs to guide visitors through wildlife management areas all over Florida, and down river trails—the Aucilla, the Wacissa, Lake Lafayette, even the floodplain creeks of the massive Apalachicola. What a great job this is, I'd think, when the projects required ground truthing and carving trails in the field. But most days, I was locked at my desk behind a plate glass window. The maps and pictures I was drawing in people's minds began to feel too small, especially when I tried to factor in the biggest possible stressor—climate change.

One day, my work took me to Hagen's Cove on the Big Bend coastline south and east of Tallahassee. My assignment was to create several sign panels that would introduce visitors to that remote and beautiful landscape. Jeff had come along to keep me company.

What could I write to capture the essence of the Tide Swamp Wildlife Management Area? The area manager (my usual source for interpretive messaging) had been called off to manage a prescribed burn and couldn't offer his counsel. So it was just us and the cove, finding our way toward what stories offered themselves. A sloshing low tide and a single bald eagle perched on a silver skeleton of a cedar tree caught my eye when I slid the truck into the gravel lot.

We stepped from the vehicle and my boots sank into the pocked sand, even though the wrack line of the tide was hundreds of yards to the west. No better place in Florida to grasp the concept of flat, I thought, flipping open my notebook to an empty page.

We stood in silence, breathing in the salt wind, and the place begin to talk. Cabbage palm fronds rattled; blackbirds and grackle creaked like rusty gates. What was the real story here? What words could I employ to sharpen a visitor's focus if she stood in my shoes? What brief bursts of text and simple images might open her mind to match the expanse of this horizon?

I faced west, toward the water, ignoring for the moment the pine flatwoods and wetland forests at my back. The old-growth cypress and virgin pines had been logged away and shredded long since, their green memory turned to dollars and smoke. Industrial pine plantations had been seeded into the swampy ground like crops of cotton or corn. Now my agency had undertaken a slow restoration of the landscape into a place where wild things might once again live.

It was an essential and lovely tale—land acquisition and restoration—but I'd written it for other protected management areas, at Three Lakes and Hickory Mound and Fisheating Creek. What else could we notice at just this edge, this cove, this coast? Nowhere is static on this Earth, even when purchased and finally protected. What was unique to this stretch of Gulf Coast borderlands? My eyes rested on the broad marshes. A tourist might stop at this empty place on the map with a certain expectation of the edge of Florida, particularly white beach. But instead of crashing waves and a crystal shingle of sand, she would find ribbons of tidal creeks coursing to the continental shelf. If it were low tide, as it was right now, she would see that shelf with her own eyes. She would find reddish egrets and white pelicans in January and an abundance of scallops in the seagrass come the summer months. Beautiful.

My pen began to play across the page.

"How about this, Jeff?" I proposed. "Wide Open and Wild. Florida's Big Bend Is a Different Kind of Coast."

"Sounds like a start," he said.

We listened to the talk between the wind and the place. There was more to tell. I hoped Hagens Cove would be a forever refuge, free from human intervention. It had already borne enough. Would that be true, though? Was it completely safe, even now?

The tourist might see how the high returning tide would pile vertically and rush far, far ashore. I studied the forest fingering into the Gulf—cabbage palm, slash pine, red cedar, live oak, yaupon holly—and the welter of hammocks perched on lime rock, rising from the needles of salt marsh. I began to see a pattern of dead and dying trees intermixed with those still living.

"What's killing those trees, do you think?" I asked Jeff. He'd been studying the landscape too, through the lens of his work as a geoscientist.

"I was just thinking about that," he answered. He kicked his boot against the barren trunk of a dead cedar. "This coastline might actually be at the leading edge of climate change in Florida." Because of the low elevation of Hagens Cove—sea level low—and its extremely gentle slope, Jeff postulated that a rising sea level forcing saltwater intrusion was behind the murder of the coastal forest.

No doubt about it. For the interpretive materials at this site, I'd have to talk about climate change. I'd have to talk about sea level rising.

Three years into his diagnosis, my father began to forge a new path, his own path, through a small stand of woods. Single-minded and slow, he'd set out from his house, wending around an artificial lake and then home again, nearly every day. Midway through that mile, he'd cut off on a short looping trail next to the road and walk through a tiny tract of remnant pine barren. The dirt path was uneven and rugged, Mary Jane told me, and she worried that Dad would trip and fall. She wanted him to keep to the pavement. But I loved thinking about my father moving through that patch of native turkey oak and sand pine. I felt that the tender sandy soil welcomed his quiet feet and that the trees appreciated his attentions.

Dad picked up trash as he walked, discarded cans and condoms, bottles and food wrappers left by construction workers on lunch break, young lovers, or anglers, he didn't know who. He just hauled it out. When I visited, I would help him hoist something out of the woods that he hadn't been able to manage alone. One time he kept an eye on an old battery, counting the days until I would come and back my rental car up to the trailhead. When I did, we lifted that battery between us and drove it to a recycling center. Sometimes over the phone, he'd tell me he was giving it up, that he couldn't keep pace with the refuse accumulating on his trail. But he never did stop. Not of his own accord.

My father's patch of trees was probably doomed. Construction in the retirement community inched ever closer, from west to east. I didn't want to investigate when that land might be slated for the bulldozer. I couldn't bear to contemplate a time when Dad's tiny trail might go under blade and saw and he would lose the connection with that little bit of nature still accessible to him. But my father's body fell before those trees ever did.

CHAPTER 4

Wildlife 2060

I found my dad in room 301 of the intensive care unit of the Atlantic City Medical Center. He lay very still in the bed and didn't respond to my greeting. Mary Jane sat in a chair beside him, no bigger than a crumpled pile of clothes. "They gave him morphine at six forty-five this morning," she said. "He's in quite a bit of pain. We can ask for it every three hours." I squeezed in beside my stepmother on the hospital chair, wrapped my arms around her.

Dad's right forearm and wrist were wrapped in gauze, and flecks of brown blood clung to the hairs of his arm. A plastic bag hooked over the bed rail contained a small amount of extremely dark urine. Mary Jane listed the injuries he had sustained when the car hit him: broken wrist, fractured hip, multiple abrasions.

A nurse slipped into the room and inflated the blood pressure cuff on my father's left arm. "It's 149/70," she said. "That's good. When he was here alone yesterday it was significantly higher. Family calms him down." She smiled at us.

Outside our room, clusters of people periodically emerged from the elevator. All of a sudden there they'd be, hovering in the doorways of the wounded people they loved. I'd learn over the next week just how many of Dad's fellow intensive care patients had been injured by cars. So many that it felt like there was a war going on: cars against humans. The humans appeared to be losing.

And not only people were going down. Between Atlantic City and Manahawkin, between Tallahassee and Crawfordville, anywhere I drove my car, devastating stretches of For Sale signs marked the trees, signaling an economic conversion of the land to human constructs that boggled my brain. I felt almost as crazy passing by the bulldozers pushing down live trees as I did witnessing the damage done to my father's body. All of it beyond my control. A quarter acre of swamp traded for a dollar store. Forty acres of pine woods buried under a Walmart. A hip fractured on asphalt. What am I here for if I can't save or protect a single place or thing? Or person?

On the second morning of Dad's stay in intensive care, the nurses moved him into a large, padded lounge chair. Good, I thought, that looks like progress. At least he was resting in a different position. We began to tend to him, my sister, Mary Jane, and I, and he looked more himself once we'd shaved his face and neck and hooked his glasses over his ears.

"Who are all those little fellows?" he asked, sight restored. There was no one but us in the room.

"Do you mean children?" I asked. I caught on to his confusion and didn't correct him.

"All about five years old," he said. "They are probably yours, Sue." After a pause he asked, "What does it say on that young fellow's chest?"

"You mean on his sweatshirt?" It was easy to enter his delusion, but that didn't mean I could read the logo on the unseen boy's garment.

"Then there's the dog," Dad continued, picking at his bandaged wrist with his good left hand.

"What breed?" What else could I say?

"It's tall," my dad confided.

"Is it a German shepherd?" I imagined my way into his confusion, remembering the dogs we'd had as children.

"Probably," said Dad. "That was one mistake our family made: all those lousy dogs."

He moved on to the subject of his nurses. "Is that Danish one immigrating?"

The nurse answered for herself: "I'm not going anywhere, Mr. Isleib, but we will probably get you back in bed soon."

Dad replied: "And that will solve everything, won't it?"

"I'm so discouraged, Sue," he said, after he'd been transferred back into the bed. I couldn't tell him everything would be okay. His mind was returning, but his body had lost more ground.

But as the shock of the accident and the surgeries receded, Dad began to eat again. After two rounds of cereal, seafood chowder, a third of a chicken breast, chunks of pineapple and cucumber, and a carton of coffee yogurt, he progressed to questions. Where was his cane, where was his wallet, and where were his damn glasses? My sister and I stayed on in Atlantic City, day after day, a week, caring for him physically as we could and supporting Mary Jane. My youngest sister, Martha, drove up from North Carolina to visit, and then our brother, Doug, from Maryland. Dad's brother, Don, was constantly calling one of our cells for updates.

Dad dreamed that he and I were attending Spanish classes. Not so surprising, because in the hospital bed by the window, a young Hispanic boy lay behind a cloth curtain. We had watched his parents pass in and out the door at the foot of Dad's bed, but they spoke no English, and we had no Spanish. The best we could do was to exchange smiles.

Dad caught the father's eye. "*Buenos días!*" he called from his bed. "*Me llamo Bob.*" The other man smiled, pointed at his own chest. "Candido," he said, introducing himself. Magdalena, his wife was called. I had noticed how infrequently she left the room, how frail and worn she appeared. Candido pulled back the curtain and formally introduced their son, Ricardo, as if the young man could hear and respond. We learned that Ricardo was twenty-one and that his brain had been badly damaged when he was hit by a car, like Dad, while walking. Candido indicated his son's broken leg, set in a cast. He pointed to the sky, folded his hands in prayer, and pantomimed while speaking in his own language that his son's fate was now in the hands of Jesus. Our Spanish was too limited to further converse. We held our hands over our hearts, all five of us, knowing that each would pray for the other's wounded loved one.

The third morning in Atlantic City, we found Dad agitated, incoherent, and crying out in pain. I waved a nurse in from the hall and insisted that she check his chart. The night nurse had recorded that he hadn't administered Dad his pain meds, since he couldn't articulate that he hurt.

"Percocet—*right now!*" ordered my brother, an ex-marine. We knew the chart called for pain medication every three hours. "Makes me feel like we can't leave him alone night or day," I said to my siblings as we huddled around the bed.

Ricardo was in crisis too, even deeper than Dad.

"What's his white blood cell count? Blood pressure? Heart rate?" A crowd of nurses and resident doctors moved in and out of his cubicle. Machines beeped, and carts with life-saving equipment were pushed through the door. Candido and Magdalena were forced to our side of the room by the throng working around

Ricardo's bed. A Catholic nun in full regalia stood with the boy's parents, translating and attempting to comfort.

By nightfall, Ricardo had been transferred to a higher level of care: we couldn't guess at his fate. The beige curtain divider was pushed open wide. For the first time, we could see out the window. In the dark night a giant red neon sign blinked BALLY, the name of a hotel I'd passed as I walked to the boardwalk to glimpse the ocean.

Mary Jane clicked on the news. A weather forecaster reported that a big snowstorm was bearing down on South Jersey from the west. Dad's floor of the hospital would very shortly be tending to the results of two car accidents on the icy roads, and I would hear the nurses talking in the hall: "two people dead, one here in intensive care, one walked away."

Five days later, I drove Mary Jane back home to Manahawkin to prepare for Dad's hospital release. After we unpacked, I stepped out the front door of their house, drawing the cold December air deep into my lungs. What a relief from the warm stuffy climate of the hospital! I set out on a fast walk along my father's path. The lake was clear of ice. Fifteen Canada geese and a pair of mallards floated in the chill winter sun. Much of the snow dumped earlier in the week had vanished, but still I kept to the road to avoid the wet grass.

Unexpectedly, I came upon the scene of the accident. Orange spray paint marked the asphalt where the car had hit Dad. Another set of painted brackets indicated the terribly distant spot where his body came to rest on the road. I could feel the shock of the blow in my body. I made out tire marks in the frozen mud where emergency vehicles had parked as well.

We all knew it wasn't the car's impact that brought on my father's dementia. Nevertheless, the accident had caused him to endure enormous pain, would hasten his mental slide, and would soon cost him a life lived at home.

"How about helping us put together a new report on predicted wildlife habitat loss in Florida?" The voice on the phone belonged to a respected wildlife biologist in my agency with special training in the management of black bears. "We need someone who can translate our data into simple language that anyone can understand."

"Right up my alley, I'd be glad to help," I replied.

"We'll meet next Monday at 2:00 p.m. in the Bryant Building, second floor," he said. "Appreciate it!"

The agency's headquarters had changed very little since I was hired to work there in the mid-1980s. In the meeting room, a group of biologists and commission staff had gathered around a long set of conference tables. Photographs of the five current commissioners hung on the wall; I didn't know any of them now, but their framed images transported me for a moment to my beginnings here, half a life ago. Back then, it was rare for a woman to rise in these ranks. Most of the staff were white men with traditional training in wildlife biology from Auburn, Georgia, Oklahoma, or the University of Florida. The men and women in the room today were more diverse, and I knew several had degrees in marketing and advertising. They talked about audience. Who is the audience we hope to read this report? Who's got the power to make the changes we need to see? And, how can we communicate to these folks what we think they need to know?

As the biologists led us through the data they wanted to impart to Floridians, the potential landscape-level losses facing our state staggered me. I couldn't imagine language or images powerful enough to help people understand and decisively act. The facts were not in dispute; the agency's senior scientists were known to be cautious and measured with their numbers. I wondered: Didn't those data make them crazy? I didn't know how we could possess this information and still remain seated around the conference table without issuing a collective wail of mourning and despair. But not one person made a sound.

I knew that each of us was looking for an end to the dichotomy, the dysfunction of our human minds, that allows our human population to believe that we can use up all the freshwater and natural lands, all the natural resources, and that life would proceed as usual. It was as if we were being swept down a very swift river, with thousands of new people moving to Florida, flooding and sprawling over the landscape that wild creatures need if they are also to live. Within the last one hundred years, we humans have shifted from a species with mostly local influence to one that dominates all life on our planet. And even as we have increased exponentially in numbers and technological reach, the drive to consume resources still runs us. It wasn't the job of the state wildlife agency—conservative, ponderous, earnest—to stem that tide, but offering the facts, yes, that they could do. Even though I worked there only part time now and anticipated the day I'd finally resign and write exactly what and how I chose, I wanted to join those colleagues in presenting a longer view to the state's residents and decision makers.

Back in my office, I wrapped my hands around a mug of spiced tea and considered my task. I watched a family of gray squirrels rocket and spiral around the trunk of a laurel oak tree just outside the broad window over my desk. I couldn't hear the squirrels chatter nor the tear of their claws on tree bark. But I knew those sounds, and I smiled, watching the family of small mammals at play. I propped my feet on the bottom drawer of my desk and leaned back in my chair and reflected on the burden of being conscious and the great inevitable sorrow of seeing and understanding the losses. I watched a tiny blue-gray gnatcatcher gleaning the oak leaves outside and I had a sudden desire to simply be an animal, to just live, to follow all the burning and blind urges of a simple existence, not to see the "big picture," only to orient to the great sun and the green leaf. To be innocent. Not to know about, or in any way to have caused, the destruction we are imparting on our planet.

I flipped through the data the biologists had asked me to interpret. The scale of predicted loss was unimaginable, even crazy. Maybe the right word was *demented*. How else to explain the devastation we faced over the next fifty years? With the predicted influx of eighteen million new residents to Florida, competition between wildlife and humans for land and water resources would be intensely heightened. Seven million additional acres of land—equivalent to the state of Vermont— could be converted from rural and natural to urban uses. Nearly 3 million acres of existing agricultural lands and 2.7 million acres of native habitat will be claimed by roads, shopping malls, and subdivisions.

As I contemplated that loss, the squirrels in the oak tree continued to play. They seemed to live in a different universe from me in my office, a world beyond fixed glass. Most of us humans are just as divided from the place we live. We no longer believe we even share the same air as the wild things that lived "outside." We have been lulled into thinking that our destinies, our very survival, are independent of theirs and that we are safer in conditioned spaces behind panes of glass.

I watched the squirrels chase across the centipede grass in the median of the parking lot. Gray squirrels can always make a life in such minimal habitat, so long as there is grass and acorns and a few branches where they might build a nest. I thought of another species of squirrel native to Florida much less likely to survive our incursions.

The fox squirrel. I'd seen one a week or two earlier, trapped between a mile of tall chain-link fence and the four-lane highway near our airport. The squirrel's home—a roomy stretch of pine forest—had just been clear-cut and carted to a mill. That rare squirrel with its glossy black face and tail and graceful gait, twice as big as its common gray cousins, was doomed to bound along the roadside until it was crushed by a car. The animal could not scale the fence and there was nothing behind the chain-link left to live in, were it able.

This is the face of loss behind every For Sale sign, every new condominium complex, every new strip mall. Animals die. They cannot move elsewhere. I knew I couldn't rescue that animal, and my car and my lifestyle and I were part of the machine driving it off its land. To that squirrel, I could offer no deliverance. There was nothing I could do except grieve.

CHAPTER 5

Simulation: The Answer Is Not

My dad was pulled up to a small table in his wheelchair all by himself. He wore a tweedy blue turtleneck, sweatpants, and a deep frown like a preschooler, the one other kids don't understand and don't want to sit beside because he can't hide how he feels. His shoulders were hunched, and his face was mapped with worry. He didn't see us yet, my son David and I, standing just inside the doorway. On the wall beside us was a bulletin board peppered with announcements. One of the flyers, printed in a looping script on lavender paper stock, invited us to a workshop on the topic of "How to Have a Meaningful Visit."

Across the room, the residents of Oceanhaven Nursing Home were circled around a television in wheelchairs. A few sat on a sofa by the wall. Each patient was fitted with a silver metal clip that linked their clothing to a beeper on their chairs. As we watched, a resident tried to leave her chair. Her beeper startled.

"Rosa, sit down. Sit down, Rosa," an aide called from across the room. Rosa remained on her feet until the aide pressed her back into her seat and reset her alarm.

Dad wasn't trying to stand. His body was configured into a series of four right angles in the wheelchair: head and spine, hips to knees, knees to ankles, feet. I'd never seen him so frozen.

"Sue!" he exclaimed as we approached, and his eyes embraced me and David too, my tall and beautiful son, now seventeen years old. The look on my father's face reminded me of picking up David from kindergarten, how he would light up when he saw me coming across the room. If you stepped in between us, mother and son, and now, father and daughter, you'd feel the fire of our love and want to warm yourself beside it. Only back then, David didn't look so worried, and now, my dad did.

"Where have you been?" A mix of tamped-down panic and joy spread across his face. "I nearly had to resign from this place this morning. You're not your own man here."

Resigning wasn't an option, of course. He was still recovering from the multiple injuries he'd suffered in November.

We chatted about the college tour David and I were just beginning.

"Here's our itinerary, Grandpa," David said, describing our ambitious spring break travel. "First, we'll visit Princeton, then spend the night at Aunt Bobbie's. She'll tour us around the campus of Yale, and then the next day we'll drive out and see Brown University, then Amherst, and end up at Wesleyan, in Connecticut."

Dad nodded and began to relax. I watched his spine grow taller. He transformed into wise-Grandpa, Grandpa-who-has-seen-the-world. "You know, those are all very good schools," he said to my son. "But you don't want to get yourself into too much debt."

We wheeled Dad around the right angles of his unit: four sides of a square. A wide linoleum corridor divided the patients' rooms from the dining area.

In Dad's room, David and I tried to follow the nursing home protocol posted above the bed: *Take the foot rest off the wheelchair. Encourage patient to press hands into the chair arms, push up to standing, and edge back against bed frame. When knees contact bed, sit down, lie back, swing legs into bed, remove shoes and socks.* But Dad couldn't comply. All we could manage was to coax him up from the chair into a semicrouch over the bed.

"How about if I just plummet into the sheets," he said, and down he went, face forward, with me holding on to the waist band of his blue sweatpants. David and I flipped him onto his back like a pancake, shifted his legs toward the foot of the bed, and squared up his head and shoulders on the pillow.

His eyes flew open. "But where will you two sleep tonight?"

"Mary Jane has beds ready for us," I told him, hoping that he wouldn't protest our leaving to sleep at his own home, the place he wanted to return to more than anywhere in the world. But he was too exhausted to struggle. "Goodnight," he murmured.

When David and I walked out into the cold night, fresh air rushed over our skin, carrying the breath of salt marsh and sea. I inhaled deeply, letting the wind empty my lungs of nursing home odors. I linked arms with my son.

"Mom, this is a terrible place for Grandpa to be!" said David, looking back over his shoulder at the bright lights of the facility. He was right. Dad was stashed at a high cost in a place he disliked, a place where he had no cherished friends. But months had passed since that careless driver had tossed him from his life, fracturing his ankle and pelvis on the asphalt road. He was still frail as a pinkie mouse. We could see that for ourselves. We hoped against hope that Oceanhaven, a rehab facility nothing like his home, was just a necessary stepping stone toward returning to his real life.

From my bed in Dad and Mary Jane's small guest room, I listened to my son rustling the sheets as he settled into a mattress upstairs in his grandfather's loft office. Not so long from now, David would go off to college, returning to my house, not to live, but only to visit. I would make up his bed with soft flannel sheets, as Mary Jane had done for us today. As Dad once did, when he was able. I could not imagine and I did not want to dwell on that loss.

The next morning, we drove through the sun-yellow spring day with Mary Jane to pick up Dad from Oceanhaven. First we unloaded a lightweight, wheeled walker we'd purchased. Dad was pleased. "I have this dream that I will strike out boldly with this new equipment." He knew that going home depended on strengthening his body.

"Let's give it a test drive," I said. "After you do a few circles around these halls with the new walker, we will go visit that forest you like out at Batsto State Park."

He said, "I can hardly wait!"

And we did. It was so golden there: the just-unfolding leaves, the orioles and pine warblers and great-crested flycatchers, a dusting of oak pollen. We found a picnic table to spread out our snacks and sat among those birds, our family contained by all that beauty, breathing in the real air, the unmodulated temperature and humidity, the light. Dad said, "Isn't this just grand? This is heaven on Earth!"

And that night he dreamed about going back out to Batsto: the baby leaves of the trees, and all the birds we heard, and the four of us sitting together for a timeless span. He dreamed that David got into the college he most yearned to attend and that my sister Martha was happy in her job.

What I didn't want was for our brief visit to be the exception in my father's last years alive on the planet. The facility manager had outlined the psychological protocol for caring for patients with dementia to me and Mary Jane. Stimulate the memory and the senses.

"We use these flash cards," she enthused, as she flipped through the images in her deck. A bus, a kitchen, a cradle. "On Tuesdays at 10:00 a.m. we offer chair stretches, sometimes a ball toss." I shuddered, knowing how much my father would hate those activities. He'd know, just as I did, that this was only simulation: well-intentioned, research-solid, very expensive simulation. It made my heart hurt to think of my father stashed in an expensive facility where a cheery woman showing a flash card of an attic, asking, "Did you have an attic in your house?" was a quality of life activity. I felt sad for all of the elders whose waning days were spent in institutions where imposed routines cut them off from the things that mattered most to them in their lives.

I got to thinking about simulation and how it is also a way of life, whether you like it or not, whether you know it or not, when you visit or move to Florida's southern and coastal counties. Gated communities, strip malls, and the Disney attractions have replaced much of the real and beautiful land, hoping to sell you something they've designed and built instead. When David was very young we'd occasionally visit a theme park in Orlando. SeaWorld was the least offensive. The first time we went, we were properly eager guests, ready for the suspension of reality that the Orlando attractions demand. But by the end of the day, pummeled by heat and hard sidewalks, overstimulated by fantastic animal shows and adrenaline-pumping rides, I felt profoundly disturbed by this corporate way of "making contact with another world."

"Let's pretend we're on a treasure hunt," I said to my six-year-old son. I thought we might distance ourselves a bit, rather than simply collude with the cheerful presentation. "Let's see how many bits of native Florida we can find in SeaWorld."

A white ibis was number one on our unusual checklist. I edged within three feet of her, studying her mild blue eyes mounted above a stunning red sickle of a beak. "Look how close she is, David!" I whispered to him. She stared back at us, unafraid.

I could see how her silky white feathers were laid one on the next, just so. I admired the reptilian skin that clothed her yard-long legs. The nitrogenous odor of bird excrement stung our nostrils. This close, I could almost imagine away the black metal fence between us. This close, I could imagine I was with the ibis where she belonged, in a remote cypress swamp or a wide freshwater marsh.

"Mom, people throw money at everything!" said David. He pointed out the shiny coins that speckled the floor of the shallow pool where the ibis stood. I gave him two quarters to purchase a handful of bird food from a glass gumball machine.

Scarlet ibis from South America and pink flamingos marked with numbered leg bands competed with our white ibis for the brown niblets David scattered into their midst. A pink flamingo labeled number twenty-nine grazed the top of its head on the concrete pool bottom as it filtered pellets from the water.

In a nearby pond, we picked out a hooded merganser (out of season, but native); roseate spoonbill (year-round Florida resident, but rarely found this far inland in the summer months); common moorhen with chicks (in place and on schedule); and a female shoveler (another winter resident of Florida—should be nesting in the northern United States this time of year). A cinereous vulture from Eurasia hunkered on a tiny spoil island under a graceful willow tree.

The willow, we noted, was a Florida native. The vulture was not.

We love and care for what we have come to know through immersion, moment by moment by moment, over long intimate years. Understanding the place we live in or visit, in this way, leads us to connect and tend and defend. What has been arranged for entertainment or convenience—simulated—doesn't stick in our hearts. So we simply move through, uncommitted. If we are shown a Eurasian vulture tethered to a bit of lawn grass in central Florida, we may admire the bird's majestic size and curious features. But we will not know the bird in context, the landscape that it was born to hover over, the creatures it eats to survive, where it roosts and takes water. Here the bird is a rare and expensive specimen and we are observers, passing by and moving on. SeaWorld doesn't ask for our love, or even our loyalty. The natural world requires both.

The Orlando attractions confuse those who want to understand Florida, because in their design and construction, no value is accorded to what has come before and rooted deeply and flourished, be it native people or native plants. The proliferation of Disney and SeaWorld and all their cousins erases the wisdom of this place, the unique and resilient plants and animals that once clothed the face of our peninsula.

"Let's go see the dolphins, Mom!" David tugged at my wrist, pulling me toward a shaded stadium down the path. The interpretive signage and the trainers

Wild bottlenose dolphins belong in the wild. Photo by David Moynahan.

informed us that we were about to witness something truly genuine in this dolphin show. But as we took a seat in the bleachers, facing forward with the host of other people, it was as if we watched television or the movies together. We were voyeurs, I thought, or consumers, at the least.

David jumped to his feet as half a dozen sleek dolphins swirled into the main pool. Three young trainers, bouncy in their black-and-red wetsuits, rubbed the heads of the dolphins, fed them treats. Despite my decision to remove myself emotionally, despite the hype and the captive state of the animals, still I felt moved to tears by those awesome life forms so close to us.

But it is precisely the real world that millions of visitors are encouraged to escape in the fantasy realms of these parks. Nonstop sensual engagement ensures that visitors will not for one minute be bored and that, at the same time, they will always be safe.

On another day, in another kind of sea world, I was again moved by the presence of dolphins. We'd traveled to picnic at the western tip of St. George Island. A few hundred yards away lay a smaller island. The water passing between the two was full of power and the rising of the tide, surging as it did, from the Gulf of Mexico toward Apalachicola Bay. In its currents it carried the wild lives of uncountable sea creatures.

Some of these animals we saw: three manta rays the size of bathtubs, skimming the water's surface, powered by the flap of black wings. Pelicans and terns plunging in pursuit of small bait fish. And yes, bottle-nosed dolphins, arcing the width of the channel, a whole family group of them. No trainer choreographed that moment, no walls contained the animals, nor did—or could—proffered treats enlist their tricks. We felt no need to applaud. Every creature around us, and each of us humans, was engrossed in its own living, securely at home on Earth.

My friends and I wrestled and played with our young children in the sand, joining our human exuberance with the life of the place. The sea moved on and around us, both oblivious and fully aware. The sun dropped into the water. Chill night air rushed over our skin. There was no question that we stood on authentic ground and participated in miraculous life.

Another visit north. Mary Jane couldn't care for our father herself anymore, and the idea of sharing their small home with hired caregivers made her anxious. Dad had been moved to Seacrest, a nursing facility close to the house Dad and Mary Jane had shared, and it appeared that was where he'd remain.

On my first visit to Seacrest, the nursing home was mobilized with purpose. Every resident moved in the same direction, such as they were able. Mary Jane and I wheeled my father to the big sunny dining room on the third floor. The windows were wide open to the glorious spring day; light and air filled the room, and on stage was Gino Valente, an entertainer all the way from Atlantic City. This was a rare event for the residents of Seacrest, a mini–rock concert. The aides passed out hot chocolate chip cookies on Styrofoam plates. Mary Jane and I had been seduced by the aroma of those cookies baking as we'd made our way through the halls.

Gino Valente was tethered to a long microphone cord, which allowed him to rove about the room in his black blazer and clean white Rockport sneakers. His eye contact was impressive.

"Dean Martin sure was a class act, wasn't he?" asked the singer. Several in the audience nodded and murmured in agreement. "But you know where *he* ended up, don't you?"

"Japan?" someone guessed.

"No!" Gino laughed. "The nuthouse!" He moved right into Dean Martin's trademark "That's Amore." Gino's son-in-law supported the singer's honey-lovely voice with a background orchestra on an iPod and an amp. I thought the quality of the music rising behind the old performer's voice was really quite good.

His second selection, a seductive "Strangers in the Night," set the three ladies at the front table swaying and singing with open and outstretched palms, as if receiving a gift.

But my dad ignored the music. I watched him scowl at a woman dressed in plastic pearls and bubblegum-pink nail polish. Her hair was cut severely short and she wore it tucked behind her ears.

"That one thinks she's a man," he told me. "And she doesn't try to hide it." She did look a little butch, but I hadn't known that to bother my father before.

The lady on my right clutched her elbows against her beige sweater, rocked in her red faux leather wheelchair to a love song about a one-way trip to the sun. I watched her run her hands over the plastic tabletop, as if to smooth a cloth, or the length of a child's dress. My heart hurt and my eyes filled, but it wasn't until Gino laid into Louis Armstrong's "What a Wonderful World" that I thought I might break down. I had to turn away from my stepmother, Mary Jane, who wept openly as she sang out the words. Between us, Dad held himself back, impassive to the music he'd once so loved. I surveyed the dozens of people parked in that spring-brilliant space, people who had lost almost everything—home, independence, spouse, and children—and some of them, their minds. And I wondered if this were a case where gorgeous music evoked more pain than pleasure. At least for my dad, I thought, that might be true.

A few days later, I reached him on the phone: "I finally have been able to come up with a word to describe how I feel," said my father. I held my breath on the other end of the line, wondering what he'd reveal.

"Homesick," he said. "Just that." Never going home again, living in a place and with people he didn't know or choose, that he didn't want to face.

"I am looking for ways not to despair," he said.

Wildlife festivals were one of the ways my colleagues and I were trying to help people experience the real Florida, not just the attractions. I traveled downstate to Glades County, finding my way to a public facility in the tiny town of Moore

Haven, population 1,500. A pleasing wind blew through the planted palms lining a vast parking lot, and beyond the rustle of their fronds, enormous cargo trucks rolled past.

"How many people have registered for the festival?" I asked Tracie. I'd located my hostess among the vendors offering local barbecue, cotton candy, and kettle corn. We'd met at a Watchable Wildlife conference in Fort Myers a year earlier, and she'd invited me to keynote tiny inland Glades County's first birding festival.

"Only twenty-six," she replied, dragging deeply on her cigarette, her voice raspy and low. "I'm hoping we'll have a lot of walk-ins." Judging by the frequency of her smokes, Tracie was even more nervous than I was. She seemed to be waiting—or hoping to conjure—carloads of bird-watchers to her event. It was an unusual pairing for rural Glades County, the idea of selling bird-watching, the beginnings of ecotourism.

A decade or more ago, I'd spent time here working up an entry for the *Florida Wildlife Viewing Guide* with my friend Ann Morrow. We'd come up with the concept of the Lake Okeechobee Scenic Trail, which directed wildlife watchers to the seminatural dry prairies and palm savannas on the west side of the lake, where crested caracaras, sandhill cranes, and swallow-tailed kites still thrived. Particularly drawn by those kites, I'd returned to Glades County over and over, to track their journeys and write my second book. I knew I'd never make money doing it, but that's what Glades County wanted, and what Tracie needed to make happen, if nature-based tourism was to succeed in this rural part of Florida.

Inside the auditorium, purveyors of cheap jewelry, wind chimes, and bird baths offered their products on tables lining the auditorium walls, interspersed with the exhibits of local conservation groups. I visited my friends from the Great Florida Birding Trail, the Corkscrew Swamp Sanctuary, and the Audubon Center for Birds of Prey. Two empty perches promised a display of live birds later in the evening.

On the registration table, amid a swirl of giveaway plastic pens and local advertising brochures, I fanned a couple dozen glossy postcards featuring my book cover. *Tracking Desire: A Journey after Swallow-Tailed Kites* side by side with "Glades County: We Have Room for Your Business!" Was this really going to work?

My friend and co-keynoter, the nature photographer John Moran, blew through the double glass doors with boxes of his wares in his arms. I whispered a quick update, "Only two dozen people so far!" and he calmed me.

"Let's think of ourselves as festival hosts and take this really seriously," he said, "no matter how many people show up." John's business cards were shrink-wrapped copies of his better-known images: a host of alligator eyes gleaming in a central Florida lake, palm islands off the Big Bend Coast, Ichetucknee Springs. He gave a dozen to the woman accepting door prize contributions. I felt stingy in comparison (how can a writer make any money at all, if not by selling her books?), so I signed a copy of *Tracking Desire* and added it to the pile of freebies.

The aroma of dinner cheered me, even though, ironically, we were about to sample a feast of local wildlife: fried gator tail, venison, and softshell turtle stew. I loaded my plate with a cold black-eyed pea salad fired with raw rings of jalapeno pepper and a luscious corn pudding. Khaki-clad Audubon folks delivered a reha-bilitated bald eagle and a crested caracara missing half a wing to the perches, and it began to feel like a real opening night.

A small but lively crowd had flocked to the free bar: all the wine, beer, or mixed drinks you could imbibe. I overheard Tracie say to a coworker, "I'm so bummed by the low turnout. I'm going to call over to the county courthouse and invite any-one still at work to help us eat all this food."

John and I ferried our plates to a set of long folding tables in a darkened corner of the room. The tables were lit by battery-operated candles, which flickered and reflected off scatterings of colored glass stones.

"Where are you all from?" I determined to engage the couple across the table, our customer base.

"Ohio," said the man, friendly and full of smiles. "I'm Bill and this is Shirley, my wife."

"That's a long way to come for a bird festival." I wondered which special Glades County birds drew these two so far from home.

"Oh, we aren't bird-watchers, we run the Kountry Korn booth out in the park-ing lot," his wife explained. "What we do is sell caramelized popcorn varieties."

During the next thirty minutes, we were schooled in the ins and outs of a Florida snowbird food vendor, how every spring and summer Shirley applied to dozens of festivals across the state. And then, how all winter long, towing their booth behind a camper van, they'd zig and zag from Naples to St. Augustine. We learned that the couple began in ice cream, until their freezer lost power one night and melted thousands of dollars worth of product. "That business was a real flop," said Bill, sliding a chunk of crispy gator tail into his mouth.

I retreated to the buffet for seconds on the starches, winding through the party happening at the bar. No one had been issued a name tag, but Tracie pointed out that the bartenders included two Glades County commissioners and the mayor of Moore Haven. They were dressed sharp as movie cowboys, in tight-fitting jeans, starched pastel shirts, and tooled leather boots.

The exit doors behind the makeshift bar swung open to admit more county employees lured by Tracie's invitation of free booze. The golden rays of the equinox sun slanted for just a moment into the room, and I longed to bolt to Fisheating Creek, only ten minutes away, to watch its beautiful set. The swallow-tailed kites wouldn't be gathered in big numbers yet, but how wide and quiet would be the air and the sky!

But John said no, we needed to stay. He'd just met tonight's speaker, a shorebird enthusiast and fine artist from coastal Georgia.

"This is my first formal presentation," she confided. "I'm pretty nervous." John helped her plug in the PowerPoint projector she'd brought, but then there was the matter of a screen. There wasn't one.

Two of the festival organizers offered "to rig something up." "Not very professional," I muttered to John as we watched how, working with one hand each, gripping the lips of their red Solo cups brimming with rum and Coke, the two men pinned a wrinkled round tablecloth to a shaky wall partition.

Finally, John approached one of the men and asked if they might have a real screen in their office building two blocks away.

I didn't think the man was joking when he said, "I know we used to have a big screen to project our porn, but everyone's pretty much converted to DVDs by now."

I locked eyes with John. "We are going to have to learn to speak another language," he mouthed over the noise of the crowd. I pinched a tablecloth from one of the vendors' tables, noting that none of the jewelry for sale featured even a generic form of wildlife, and we strung it up tight, so it wouldn't wrinkle the legs of the artist's projected willets and plovers. She launched into her carefully crafted presentation, explaining how she sketched wild birds, protected them, watched them. Tracie herded the more raucous members of the crowd out the door, so that the speaker's voice could be heard. There were no questions at the end of her talk.

All the evening's disappointment and inconsistencies faded in my mind when John and I made our way to the small cabins in LaBelle where we'd spend the night. For a solid mile, we drove beneath a sky filled with spiraling swirls of tree swallows. I knew they were massed for their northward migration. At last, a true festival of birds.

CHAPTER 6

How We Are Lost

"Mom," said my son. "This is the last time we will cook together before you take me to college." David stood beside me in our kitchen, his knife thwacking through carrots, broccoli, and garlic he had laid on a wooden cutting board. My son, now eighteen, was in my heart still a child, my child. But truly, he was more man than boy, eager to get out into his own life and more present than I with what was being cut for the last time that night.

I hadn't been thinking beyond the days we still had together: our travel north to Connecticut, a celebration with my sister and brother-in-law, shopping for David's new room in the dorm, and freshman orientation. David anticipated the day after those days—the beginning of life on his own.

"Let me season the stir fry." He took the spatula from my hand and my place at the stove. It wasn't the onions spitting in the hot oil that caused my eyes to suddenly fill. With the hem of my white shirt, I wiped the steam from my glasses and the tears from my cheeks.

"Thief, thief," screamed a blue jay in the backyard. I heard its cry through the open window, and I agreed. Our old calico cat threaded between my ankles and David's on the tile floor of the kitchen. I rested my head briefly against the shoulder of my son.

"You take the window seat, David," I said, as we boarded the plane the next morning. "You'll like watching the landscape change." As we approached the Hartford airport, we could see from the window of the plane how even the light was different in Connecticut, and how in late August, the terminal leaves of the maple trees were turning yellow and red already. "This sure isn't Florida," David said quietly. "Florida is so far away."

Bittersweet farewell to son David on first day at Wesleyan University (August 2008).
Photo by the author.

The president of Wesleyan University told us he hoped our children would find challenge and passion in the four years to come. In the dark and lovely chapel, we listened to him speak, parents and freshmen children together. In the pew beside me, a man sat so still it was as if his feet were nailed to the pine-planked floor. Eyes cast down, he kneaded his knees with his hands, as if they were loaves of bread. I wondered if he was running films in his mind—of the years raising the daughter from whom he would soon part. Or maybe he was pondering the advice of the new parent committee: "If you don't already have a life of your own, find one. If you do, then get busy. Quit obsessing about how your child will manage her new life here at college without you." I felt the pain of impending separation rolling off his body in waves.

When we were released from the chapel back into the light, David and I ambled back to his dorm, admiring the excellent features of his new world: the student center, Foss Hill, athletic playing fields, an enormous library.

"I can't wait to meet the cocaptains of the ultimate frisbee team!" An uncommonly large grin lit his face. At the door to his room, where we had mounted a dry erase board to receive messages from the friends he hadn't yet met, we shared a long hug. And then he was gone. Off to a freshman barbecue with a yellow-haired girl from Los Angeles.

The night was dark, and Middletown, so charming when I explored its narrow, one-way streets with my son, was harsh and unforgiving of my grief. I believed I knew the return route to my sister's house in Madison, but instead I was heading west on Highway 6 to Meriden. How could this road be wrong when we had driven it together, my son and I, just hours before, when the morning was light and soft? There was the store where we bought a lamp for his desk, and a sixty-watt bulb, and a tall, vining philodendron with heart-shaped leaves for his windowsill. Without my son beside me in the night, that store was just a brightly lit barn of consumer excess. Were I to pull into the parking lot, even if I steered my rental car between the very same pair of painted lines where we had filled the car with his supplies, there would be nothing of him. For eighteen years, he had been at the very core of my life.

At a stoplight, I pressed the back of my head against the seat. Vertigo swept my body. My neck felt as if it had been whipped in circles, and the reeling would not stop. I knew I was not the only parent feeling so lost, but nevertheless, I was completely alone.

My cell phone buzzed in my pocket. I pulled off the road into the parking lot of a darkened pizzeria. The screen read "Dave," a message. I pressed the OK button. "I love you, Mom! Thanks for supporting me in this fabulous experience!" For just a moment, I absorbed the exclamation points in his message, and from my heart I wished him every good thing. Then I pulled out the small map the rental car company had provided and began to navigate my own way home.

"Honest to God, Sue, I'm so glad you called," said my dad. His words came all in a rush. "Talking to you helps ground me in reality. There's a hobo in my room. He could easily slip a knife in my gut, and I don't want to face that."

I was a thousand miles away, stacking breakfast dishes in my north Florida kitchen, when my father called. It was hard to get hold of him, unless Mary Jane was there and could help him manage the phone. The telephone stood on the bed stand and was out of his reach and beyond his abilities to use. I couldn't guess how he'd dialed me up just now.

"Why do you think Fred wants to kill you?"

"Well, he's pretty bitter about me because I can't solve his problems. He says he doesn't have a dime in his pockets. He wanted to use my phone to call his sister but then he lost his nerve. He's so damn convoluted. It must be a defect in his mind." I couldn't see Dad's face, but I understood the urgency in his voice.

I'd met this Fred, a slight old man with crow-sharp eyes, always on the move in his wheelchair, executing frequent, erratic spins and turns. I thought maybe his left arm was the weaker, because his circles generally led off to the right.

"I'll be there next week to help," I said. "But do you feel unsafe right now?"

My father didn't answer. There was a blur of talk in the background. "What's going on there, Dad?" I wiped my hands on a dishtowel, thinking I'd need to call Mary Jane or someone in charge at the facility.

"That's the nurse's aide, talking to my 'not' friend," said Dad. "It's a crazy thing around here." I knew it was. I'd seen Fred run his hands over the uninteresting contents of Dad's nightstand, looking off into the distance like a raccoon washing a crayfish. His obsession seemed less with acquisition and more about glitter or distraction. Or maybe he was looking for something he had lost: his car keys, I wondered? Like my dad, the only thing on that old man's mind was getting out of that place.

Fred was causing trouble on the floor, and he wouldn't be staying at Seacrest much longer. The ideal patients, the ones who lasted from month to month to year, were compliant. The angry or exceedingly restless vanished. Last time I visited my father, Fred wheeled up to me, close and urgent. "Now," he said. "Help me get this straight. Once I get out of the parking lot, I turn left to get to the highway. Or do I turn right?"

"Left," I said, thinking of the two sets of locked doors that stood between Fred and his unlikely freedom. "You just turn left."

"The best I can hope for is that you all keep in touch with me. But I can't depend on my children for my sustenance," said my father before we disconnected.

Always, as I prepared to fly north, my dad would ask, "What problems will we solve while you are here?" I'd jot a list of my own priorities. Make a dentist appointment. Try to get him to his church. Push for a single room. Take him on an outing that involved fresh air and sunshine. Our Uncle Don, Dad's brother, had ideas too. Get him to a VFW meeting. Encourage old friends to visit. What about books on tape? How much we wanted to fix everything wrong with Dad's life, and how little we could actually do. He hated the rehab exercises and had lost more physical strength, even after his broken bones had knit.

My sister hired an elder care consultant to advise us further. But Mary Jane, on the front line in Manahawkin, was preoccupied with an avalanche of insurance claims from the hospital stay, the doctors, and the rehab facility, and all the legal aspects of the accident.

"Next week I have to go to a hearing with the woman who hit your dad with her car," she told me over the phone. Her voice was tight and shaky. "That woman changed her story, if you can believe it. Now she says she ran into your dad because he came into the road suddenly, from the woods, straight into her path."

But Mary Jane had arrived within minutes of the accident, and she had heard that old lady wail over and over, "I hit him, I am so sorry. I am so very sorry."

"I want it to be known. She took away the only thing he loved and still could do: his ability to walk." Mary Jane's voice was firm.

I knew she'd have no time to talk about dentists and going to church. Or even Fred.

We were perplexed by the pairing of physical frailty with Dad's relatively good mental status. When I wheeled him around the parking lot of the rehab facility, Dad said: "Look, Sue, there's a marked declivity over there," and I knew he referred to a low spot in the marsh. It wasn't a word I used and Mary Jane had never heard it before. "The air has a salutary effect on me," he said, one bright, sharp February day. Another rehab patient and his wife stopped me as I passed their table in the dining room.

"What did your Dad do 'before'?" the woman asked, referring to the constellation of ailments and accidents that had landed him in the same facility as her husband.

"He was a metallurgical engineer," I said, and she nodded.

"I thought it was something like that," she said, meaning that even though he was disabled, there was enough left to indicate the mind and body that once had been.

But when I tried to help Dad transfer to the toilet, he couldn't understand that to stand up from the wheelchair, he needed to push down with his arms and hands. Or even where to place them for leverage. Years later, we'd learn from our friend Dr. Ken Brummel-Smith, a renowned and unusually humane geriatrician, that Dad had a Parkinson's-like variant of dementia, which made sense of his symptoms, even though it couldn't be cured. I knew it affected how he was treated by the staff, especially at night.

"Most of them are kind except for a couple of real bitches," he said. I always tried to make friends, allies really, of those caregivers, and Mary Jane did too. All were very young, most extremely overweight. I'd watched them take cigarette breaks in the freezing cold, outside the glass doors of the nursing home. I learned about their children and boyfriends too. I knew their lives weren't easy.

When a raven-haired aide entered Dad's room to help him onto the toilet, he perked fully alert.

"She's one of the bad ones," he whispered to me.

As she helped him to his feet, the aide smiled and called him sweetheart.

Was this woman capable of shoving my father flat against the bed, pushing her palm against his face? I lived one thousand miles away and could be with him only a few days each month. Maybe it was too easy for me to get worked up, to pass judgment, to go indignant.

What should I do?

I reported back to Mary Jane; she surprised me by saying, "You cannot believe everything he says." When I protested, she said, "Remember that paper they showed us when we signed him up for the facility? They have zero tolerance for patient abuse." But I wondered, who's to know in the middle of the night when a frail, freaked-out patient thinks he's about to have a bowel movement and can't get in or out of bed by himself? What might any one of us do if we were an exhausted, little-paid aide, frustrated and weary, in the black of the night? It was easy for me to say, to pass judgment, to go indignant.

Bobbie and I wanted Dad to be cared for at home, with hired help for Mary Jane. But she didn't think she could tolerate all that chaos, so it appeared Dad was in assisted care facilities for good.

We daughters would come charging into town, believing that our bags of fresh peaches and our homemade blueberry pies, our roasted chickens, our transport of our father from Seacrest back into their house for a visit would ease his angst. We'd return him, ever so briefly, back into his world, and we thought we knew what was best.

One cold February day, when we wheeled Dad into the house, Mary Jane greeted us from the kitchen counter, looking so cute in pale pink slacks, a cream top, and the gold necklace Dad bought her when they traveled to Ireland, with gold earrings to match.

"My friend Ann and I do our all errands together now." Her voice was animated and lively. Even short trips to buy milk or pick up prescriptions were fun, accompanied by an able-bodied friend.

I watched Dad's face. He'd always been smitten by Mary Jane's spirit (when she wasn't bossing him around). He reached out his arms, to pull her into his lap. But she resisted his flirtations and slipped back behind the counter, busying herself with supper. Bobbie and I exchanged glances, sensing Dad's rejection.

"Let's play cribbage," I proposed, fetching Dad's homemade board and a deck of cards from the living room. "Me and Dad against Bobbie and Mary Jane." He couldn't count the cards anymore, and I never had much patience for cribbage strategy, but I figured we'd do okay together.

"One semester at University of Michigan," Dad told us, as my sister dealt the cards, "my grades slipped so badly I almost flunked out. Too much competitive cribbage and not enough studying."

"I hope to God that is all David is doing up at Wesleyan," I joked. We all roared with laughter, Dad too, Mary Jane too, knowing today's college temptations were much greater than cribbage. Mary Jane stepped to the stove, lifted the lid of a pot, then replaced it. Her eyes sparkled in the light. The room warmed with the content of family and the fragrances of made-from-scratch macaroni and cheese, steamed vegetables, and pie in the oven.

Dad looked at our three faces, one at a time, then all together, and said, "This feels kind of like home."

Mary Jane swiveled back to the stove. I saw her shoulders shake and I knew she was choking back her tears.

It must have felt like a stealth attack after dinner, how we brandished his warm red sweatshirt and struggled his arms into the sleeves. It must have felt like betrayal: forcing him into his jacket, then out into the cold night. But silently, in my mind, I was calculating the set of the sun, the fall of the dark, and the time he should be returned to the facility. And the long minutes it would take to help Dad transfer from the kitchen table to the car in the garage.

The garage was cold and smelled of old paint and pesticide. I set the brakes on the wheelchair.

"Dad, stand up and grip the top of car door," I said.

"I want to, but I can't make my body do that!" My father didn't budge. He was too heavy, too inert, for us to lift.

"Bob, get into the car!" Mary Jane's arms were crossed over her chest, and her tone carried more order than advice.

I looked at the passenger seat of the car, so close, so soft, so simple to relax into. It appeared that the act of turning and sitting was no longer in the repertoire of his brain. And yet, I thought of a certain nurse's aide at Seacrest whose touch with Dad was gentle and magically effective. I had watched her open up her arms to Dad in his wheelchair and say, "Alright now, Bob, stand up." Her voice was sweet and calm and filled with the assurance that he would meet her, and he did. He'd rise straight up into her hands. Thinking back, I know she believed in him; there was no doubt in her mind that he could do this thing, and so he did.

We didn't know what to believe about his abilities, and we were impatient and scared. When we finally hooked our elbows into his armpits and pulled him to his feet, he trembled, hunched and silent, facing the interior of the car, his body rooted to the concrete floor of the garage. It was as if he was standing his ground, what little ground there was left to stand in his life.

"Where are we going?" he asked, as I backed the rental car out of the drive. Just like his own father, my grandpa, at the end of his life, Dad lost all sense of direction when we drove around in the night.

"To Seacrest, where your bed is," I said. I couldn't bring myself to call the place where he lived "home."

"Oh, that hateful place," he said.

The next morning I awoke alone at Mary Jane's, shivering in the pull-out guest bed. My sister had left before dawn to return to Connecticut. Even a flannel nightgown and four blankets couldn't keep me warm. My hair lay flat, without body, and my skin was parched by the winter cold. But I could see outside the sliding glass doors that it had snowed in the night, so beautiful. A dry granular snow, small flaked, as brilliant as diamonds. If I couldn't fix anything today, at least I could love the snow.

In the kitchen, Mary Jane was making coffee. Wrapped in a powder blue chenille robe, she looked so tiny and vulnerable. She'd dropped weight this last year, pounds she couldn't afford to lose. I sliced cornbread from dinner the night before and slid it into her toaster oven, thinking the buttery treat might taste good to her.

At the table, she massaged her temples with her fingers.

"Another migraine?" I asked, cupping my own hands around a hot mug.

"No, just awful dreams," she replied. Dad's visit the night before had ratcheted her anxiety.

"Please tell me," I invited, slicing strawberries and bananas for our cereal.

"In the dream I had a new job in New York City. When it was time to return home, I couldn't find the right bus. Someone told me the bus I needed hardly ever came anymore. I was desperate to get back to New Jersey, but I couldn't find the way."

"Oh, Mary Jane," I said. "This whole thing with Dad is so very hard on you, isn't it? It's so difficult to know what the right things are to do. And with this progressive disease, it doesn't seem like he'll ever return to who he was."

She laid the silver butter knife carefully on her plate. My gifts of food, which meant love and comfort in my own family, didn't offer the same succor to my stepmother.

"I haven't told you kids this," she said. "I'm having panic attacks again, like I did when Stan and I first moved down here twenty years ago, and we were trying to get everything ready for our children at Thanksgiving. I thought I was definitely dying. I made Stan call an ambulance for me."

Her eyes glassed over with memory and tears.

"I do everything I can to control it . . . meditation tapes, antianxiety drugs, therapy. But last Saturday, I could barely get my car over the bridge to go to church. I forced myself to get out of the car, but I couldn't stay. I gave someone the envelope with my offering, and then I just had to go home."

"What does it feel like when that happens, Mary Jane?"

"It's like I am dying," she said. "I feel pressure in my chest, and I can't breathe. I get so dizzy. I feel like I might pass out at any minute, and I wonder if I'm going crazy."

"What helps, Mary Jane, how can I help?" I wanted so much to make things better for her. I leaned across the table and took her hand, wishing I could console her. My strategies for helping Dad hadn't fully accounted for Mary Jane's needs.

"I just need everything to stay under control," she said.

I spent that day stocking up her pantry with food. I went to Home Depot for light bulbs and Lowe's for whatever else I could check off her to-do list. I went to a greeting card store and chose the biggest, most fanciful valentine card on the rack. "For My Wife," it read, in crimson, loopy script. Because Dad did love her, so much, and yet their relationship would never again be the same, given the lopsided care forced onto Mary Jane by the changes in my father's brain and body.

In his room in the facility, I found my father holding the telephone exchanging goodnights with Mary Jane. He turned his face away from me. "Please consider my proposition—that we sleep in the same bed tonight," he pleaded. "I'd sleep well if your arm was across my chest."

He lay back on his bed with his eyes closed. I felt I was witnessing their lives at far too intimate a scale.

Dad said, "I'm just trying to figure out what's wrong between me and Mary Jane."

"Tell me more," I said.

"I'm afraid she'll have another explosion of anger if I can't do all she asks or wants me to do." He opened his blue eyes and stared straight into mine.

I showed him the Valentine's Day card I had bought for him and watched him scrawl a tiny, tiny "Bob" on the blank space at the bottom. In some ways, my father was no longer Mary Jane's husband. But to him—she was still very much his wife.

"Look, Dad," I said. "If this place doesn't work out better for you, we are just going to figure out something different." We both knew that would mean him moving to Florida or Connecticut.

"But how can I possibly arrange to live in Florida for the rest of my life?" Mary Jane still wouldn't discuss them moving within New Jersey, into assisted living together, or closer to one of her children. And my father would be lost without her frequent visits, were he to move to Florida.

"That would be traitorous to Mary Jane," he said.

My head hurt to think about it. There was no simple or right or even good and satisfying choice for him as far as living space, not that I could see.

"It would be easy enough for you to care for me on day one," Dad said. "But what about day forty?" He understood his situation better than we.

CHAPTER 7

Typical Day

On Halloween night, I watched my father tread a line of orange electrical tape glued to the floor of his room. A nurse had placed it there to help him remember the path from the toilet to his bed. In the hall, I could hear the voices of aides helping other residents prepare for sleep. Last to go would be the elders dozing in front of the television in the common area.

"Dad, I just picked up a new novel you might like. Shall I read aloud the first chapter?" I had plucked *Maisie Dobbs* from the shelves of a bookstore in Marlton, halfway between Manahawkin and the Philadelphia airport. I often stopped there on my way to Dad's, to buy a cup of tea and a cranberry scone and wander the aisles for half an hour before I faced whatever needed fixing on those visits. I thought Dad might like the World War I setting of Jacqueline Winspear's story.

After a bit, Dad settled back against the pillows. Yes, he said, the book was interesting, but he didn't think he'd be able to read it himself. "You take it home, Sue, you'll enjoy it." Was it macular degeneration or damage wreaked in his brain by ministrokes? I worried that he'd lost yet another way to divert and engage himself: reading books.

And yet he'd surprise us. Earlier in the day, he had described another resident as "garrulous." Mary Jane didn't know the meaning of the word. "It means she talks too much," my father had said. I had smiled to myself, enjoying that demonstration of his vocabulary. He could still shine.

I set the novel on the bedside table, propped my feet on the bed frame, and leaned back in the wooden chair, feeling no urgency to leave. I had helped him change into plaid cotton pajamas. The top and the bottom didn't match, but we didn't care. I began to hum, and Dad joined me, his eyes closed, unselfconscious. It was like being with David when he was small, reading and singing together in the near dark. Or was it my own childhood this night evoked, how Dad would sit on the floor between my bed and Bobbie's, holding her right hand and my left, singing together before sleep. It was something we knew how to do.

We sang songs he had taught us as children, hymns and nutty tunes that I never heard anywhere but in our home.

There's an old hollow tree, 'bout a mile here from me,
Where you lay down a dollar or two,
Then you go round the bend and you come back again
To that good old mountain dew.

And "Brightly Beams Our Father's Mercy." "Beautiful Brown Eyes" and "This Is My Father's World." When I heard the clock in the common room chime nine o'clock, I knew it was time to go.

The next morning I stopped in to see Dad before I drove north to Connecticut. The residents were eating breakfast in the dining room. A red-haired aide returned my smile and pointed to a recliner where Dad was finishing his food.

As soon as he saw me, he spoke, immediate and unguarded as a child: "Sue, I was devastated to wake up and find myself here alone at four in the morning." His eyes started with tears.

The aide placed a comforting hand on Dad's shoulder. "This is what your father eats every morning: bacon, cereal, two pieces of toast with no butter, milk, orange juice. Don't you, Bob?"

Even though I visited as often as I could and was as helpful and present as I could be when I came, it was only every six or eight weeks. And just as soon as I turned and walked to the heavy double doors of Dad's facility, pressed a four-digit code on the key pad, which no one in that memory care unit could do, I'd be released back into my freely lived life. But my father would settle back in his chair, squashed by loneliness and loss. For him, it was no comfort that I'd spent the last three days with him, because I had eventually left.

"When you are not here," the aide had confided, "your father sleeps way too much."

The next day, I walked on the campus of Wesleyan University with David. It was Parents' Weekend, and my son was leading me through his "typical" day. We sat

My dad with the first two of his four children: me (left) and sister Bobbie (circa 1953). Photo by Janet Isleib.

through two advanced classes in chemistry and microbiology. Then we walked to the cafeteria, where David ordered a chicken burrito. "This is typically what I have for lunch, Mom," he said. I was so happy to follow his lead. With our trays, we threaded through the indoor tables and chairs with our trays to a sunny deck. "This is where I typically eat lunch," he said.

I smiled at my son, at the preciousness of these two short days together. From across the quad, chapel bells rang the noon hour. Unbelievably, the song they chimed I had sung with my father just two nights before. "Brightly beams our father's mercy, from the lighthouse ever more."

I needed that lighthouse, I needed some kind of guiding beam, for grief again gripped me when the weekend was over and I left David at his dorm. Again I cried. If my father allowed himself, I knew that's what he'd do too, each time we said goodbye. I thought of my own college experience, how peripheral my parents had seemed to me at that time in my life. Their attempts at staying connected sometimes annoyed me. But that was at the time of my mother's spiraling depression, the years when she drank to self-soothe. Surely David had less reason to want to escape family and home?

My airplane cut through a haze of clouds portending snow. Far below, I glimpsed the great rivers of Connecticut and then New Jersey. Soon I'd be back in my own home, leaving Dad in a wheelchair, melancholy, and David at college, full of joy. I thought about how my plane trips divided my life from theirs like a knife slicing a cake, severing me from a time when my family was whole and together. I knew what their typical days looked like now. How should my own be molded?

Several days later, I sat in a circle of five close friends. Once a month, we gathered together to share our dreams and offer each other emotional support. I brought this dream into the circle.

I stood on the deck of a huge ferry boat cabled to an enormous dam. The dam enclosed a vast body of water, a reservoir, a safe place. But my boat was anchored to the down-stream side and I noticed that the ropes binding the ferry to the dam were thin and had begun to unravel. I knew what kind of ropes should have secured the boat: huge, thick, marine-grade cables. But these were not. The sky boiled with thunderclouds, signaling the approach of a huge storm. What would hold my boat in place?

"It's so, so hard to see David move off into his own life without me, even though he's thriving and I know it's right!" I told my friends. I knew the dream was about David, about my feelings of loss now that the physical ties that bound us had been severed.

My friends nodded. Each one was a mother herself. Each had felt the same unavoidable pain.

"Holding on, letting go, it's an incredible dream image," Mary Beth spoke first. "It really mirrors the thinning of your physical connection to your son." If anyone understood forced separation, it was this beautiful friend whose own daughter, Claire, had died at the age of fourteen.

"On the physical plane, yes," said Amrita. Her own two boys still lived at home. "I can feel what a weight your heart carries, Sue. To be cut loose from the mooring of your life together feels unbearable. But remember, in the spiritual life, whenever something painful is presented to us, we are being asked to grow, to stretch beyond the confines of who we've believed ourselves to be." I relaxed against the back of my chair. Tears flowed over my cheeks.

Crystal took my hand and added her thought. "Sue, you are in one of life's biggest transitions." Her eyes met mine, swelling with compassion. "But even when

David still lived here in Tallahassee, sometimes he felt emotionally distant to you, remember? Sometimes your relationship with him felt unavailable."

"But it wasn't true then, Sue, and it isn't true now," she cried. "Nothing can ever destroy your deep mother/son connection. Nothing can ever destroy the love between you!"

Even as the bond with my son seemed stretched so thin that first fall he was away, the umbilical cord binding me to the natural world pulled tighter than ever. My own typical days were deeply in flux. I didn't know what my next project would be, but I knew I would grow into it, walking alone in wild places. I decided it was time to leave the agency that had comfortably held me for most of two decades and find my way more deeply into my own writing voice.

All those years I had worked in an office, I had dreamed of more hours and days and weeks outside in the larger home that held me, which holds every one of us more securely than any physical structure we might build: our planet, the only place we can live. It was time to return to the big sky at the coast, with its many birds. Then I would know how to speak.

So I began: watching birds at Bald Point, swimming in the Ochlockonee River, kayaking on Buckhorn Creek, taking notes, and listening for direction. On a day in November, I drove to the state park on St. George Island. The parking lots and picnic pavilions were empty, and the Gulf horizon spread vast. I walked and walked, losing my thoughts in the motion of the green bodies of the waves. They'd rush toward shore, iced with foam, and then drown again in the gem-clear Gulf. The reliable roar of the surf calmed my brain, and I lost myself in the largeness.

The tide was low when I arrived. Ghost crabs constructed their kingdoms on the expansive shingle of the shore. Over the course of hours, the tide rose, corseting all of us species—shorebirds, crab, and human—against the grasses and oats growing on the dunes. The day's tidal range reminded me of the larger geological rhythms of the planet and how the seas were rising and would continue to do so. I knew there was nothing more important to address. I didn't know exactly what my next project would be, but I knew I would grow into it, walking alone in wild places.

PART II

I Have Been Assigned the Single Bird

The dream I had was this:
tide to dune, I walked beside the sea where
crowds spread blankets and chairs
played with their dogs and their children
built sandcastles.

Improbably, I saw
ancient claimants of the shore
dart among them
seeking space
a snowy plover and its toothpick-legged chick.
no one saw.

In the dream, I was instructed:
Don't take your eyes off that chick-child and parent!
Care for them! Protect them!

But how?
How would I keep them safe?

Far away on a deserted shore
enormous flocks of snowy plovers thrived
I wanted my job to be steward of that sturdy congregation.
more worthy, I thought
and more possible.

but
I have been assigned the single bird

CHAPTER 8

A Contract for Home

Months passed, and then several years. Life held steady, or so it seemed.

And then, on a Valentine's Day, Mary Jane died of a massive stroke. Just like that, she was gone. Abruptly, unexpectedly, forever. Even as we grieved, we worried about caring for our dad. Someone needed to assume his wife's role as advocate for our father. I knew I was the one. My sister Bobbie would help me, and it would be a chance for my brother, Doug, and me to spend more time together.

"If you will just drive Dad down here to Florida, Jeff and I will care for him," I had said to my brother at the funeral.

"You've got a deal," said Doug, knowing his was the easy end of the bargain.

On a late-spring evening, I waited at the edge of St. Augustine Road, pacing circles around a sign that read "The Landing." It was green-dark dusk, late spring in north Florida. Headlights of passing cars flicked over newborn leaves of oak and maple and the faces of me and my husband, Jeff. We waited. I hoped my brother and my dad would arrive before dark, and when they did, I wanted them to see us standing by the road, welcoming them home.

Half a dozen slash pines held up the sky between the Landing and apartments next door. Perhaps they had been planted in a block once upon a time, because they didn't have the widespread arms of a naturally forested space. Still, they hosted a few birds, and I would come to know their profiles well over the next four years. A great crested flycatcher shrieked, filling an empty space between those partial trees.

A pair of cardinals whispered in the dusk, and a Carolina wren. I paced around the sign, around Jeff, understanding that I stood between my old life as a cared-for daughter and my new role as daughter-protector. Taking care of my father seemed like a constructive thing to do, a reasonable contribution to our family, a bow to

the man who had raised me up. My desire to care for him came from some instinc-
tual place in my body, not from reason or duty alone. It was the right thing to do.
Bobbie had done her share and would continue to help me. My brother wasn't
interested. Our youngest sister had a big enough heart but even larger struggles of
her own. And I felt that I could prove Dad was capable of more than he had been
allowed under Mary Jane's watch. Maybe I thought that with enough resources
and kindness, I could raise him up from Alzheimer's as I had raised my son from
a baby to a man. But this was a dementia of my own, to think that I could change
the course of this disease.

And I had yet to answer the question: how does the tending of one dying old
man—his protracted dying—stack up against the urgencies of the world? Perhaps
I'd learn something by trying to fix or mend what is close at hand, those to whom I
was most closely related and deeply loved. Maybe, I thought, through this impossible task, I would learn the language of tending the world.

So here was the moment before the moment when my father became mine to
care for. Like a gasp, a quick in breath, or the nearly invisible pause when the tide
turns, like that. In the trajectory of a life lived together—parent and child—this
was the moment when our lifelong roles would reverse. Everything I would think
and do for him from now on would matter in a way it never had before. Before, I
had been one of three daughters and a son, and something of a consultant for our
dad and his wife. Now I'd be in charge of everything. Or so it felt. I was about to
learn how to be with my father's dementia, which would have only one possible
outcome, and at the same time, continue to search for a path out of the cultural
dementia afflicting the Earth.

A month earlier I'd sat across a wide polished desk from Ashley, the manager of this
assisted living facility. A sign on the wall of her office spelled out the facility's credo:
"The Landing is designed to give peace of mind. We offer a relaxed, non-institutional
environment, and an independent lifestyle filled with dignity and respect."

"My dad is so dear, a really special guy." I slid a list of medical disclosures across
her desk; I had to be honest. The young woman tucked a strand of pale blond hair
behind her ear while I composed myself. I desperately hoped the Landing would
work out for my father. Ashley seemed unsurprised at the intensity of my pitch.
"But he does have some physical limitations," I added.

I wanted the job of caring for him, I had asked for it, but suddenly, being responsible for everything in my father's new life worried me. At the beginning of Dad's illness, a good friend had recommended a caregiver's guide that laid out the progression of Alzheimer's disease in stages. Back then, in the beginning, I thought this was a disease with a timeline, that we could pace ourselves. But in New Jersey, for the past three years, Dad had been housed in a lockdown memory care unit. I felt he was capable of functioning at a higher level than he'd been allowed. If only I could find the right place, together we could prove it.

Ashley's perfect china doll features gave away nothing as she paged through the documents I'd brought. She looked up from the paper, locked eyes with me. "We would be happy to welcome your father into our Landing family." The certainty in her voice was steel.

"You mean, you will keep him . . . until the end?" I asked. "To the very end of his life? Before you've even met him?"

"The only way we will break this contract with you, once signed, is if your dad turns out violent," said Ashley. "Or if he wanders out of our facility." I wanted to kiss her hands. Dad wasn't physically capable of walking—he wouldn't wander. I prayed that we could temper the impatience he sometimes directed at the help in his New Jersey facilities.

A tear of relief dropped on the paper and blurred the ink as I inscribed my name and reserved the only unoccupied room at the Landing. Its availability meant someone else had just died and reminded me that anyone moving in would eventually pass as well. But it wasn't the thought of my father's mortality that summoned my emotions to the surface. It was Ashley's assurance that she could contain the rest of my dad's life within a safe, nurturing structure. That's all I wanted: a place close to my own home that could hold his stiffening body, soft heart, and diminished brain. Hopefully, Jeff and I could do the rest.

Ashley led me forty footsteps down a broad carpeted hall to my father's new quarters. A smooth wooden handrail ran the length of the corridor, paralleling a solid green line painted on the wall, all designed to lead aged eyes and bodies forward. Dad's room was second to last, on the left.

I peered into open doorways as we passed. Some of the residents had fashioned living spaces that reflected their lives and their tastes. Several had matched their decor to the facility's public rooms. But others had been too exhausted and worn or simply had different priorities than to create one last true home in these single rooms. That is what I wanted to do for my dad.

Through his window-to-be, I looked into a verdant patch of magnolia and pine and sweetgum. On account of all those trees, I thought we could sit in here as long as we had to, that the small forest would pull us out of the space of the room if we got to feeling trapped indoors. In April, when Dad arrived, and even into May, I knew I'd prop those windows wide. He'd have the voices of the cardinals and the nighttime frogs as companions in his living space.

As I pulled away from the Landing, contract in hand, I thought about how a home holds you in more ways than simply by walls and rooms and roof and windows. I marveled at the brilliant marketing strategy of Dad's new residence: *Come home to family.* Home is where you are welcome, always. Home is where your presence is integral. Not just your belongings, and your arrangement of dishes on shelves, more than that. Even the breath you exhale when you sleep matters. This facility seemed to promise all that, and more: *A warm fireplace. Plenty of natural light from our many windows. Splendidly landscaped courtyard.*

Jeff and I had thought through the floor plan of our own tiny house over and over again, looking for ways it might absorb both Dad's needs and ours. What worried us was that with the enforced helplessness of dementia, all the ways he once entertained his mind—reading, writing, travel, and frequent contact with many lifelong friends—those things were beyond his reach. That left only the present empty moment, and the next, and the next. That meant staring down a long, slow decline.

If we took him into our home, the chaos taking over his brain and his increasing physical and emotional needs would overwhelm us, just as we were adjusting to the last of our children leaving for college. Finding a place for him at the Landing countered some of the shame I felt, that I could not—or would not—care for Dad in our little house.

Was I signing a contract for family, as the literature claimed? I didn't think so, not really. You cannot contract for love. There's no amount of money you can pay to replace a lifetime of shared memory or history. You cannot purchase sisters or brothers or children. But if we were lucky, Dad might get some of that, anyway, and it wouldn't be because of the papers I'd just signed. I hoped the Landing would provide him a good enough approximation of home and that frequent visits from me and Jeff would fill in the gaps. I was counting on blond, tough Ashley to make Dad's life go right.

My father's parents lived their last years in a retirement home in Bradenton, in an unpretentious, three-story building built of brick. With roomy apartments and decent food, it was made purposefully gracious by its owners, the Presbyterian Church. It could have been apartment living except for the many dozens of antique wooden dressers, wardrobes, sideboards, grandfather clocks, and cedar chests that lined the halls and sitting areas, even the brief wall space between the elevators' doors. The furniture pieces must have been too cumbersome for families to ship back to the North or Midwest after their old relatives died, or maybe there was no one left to claim them. They resembled the cast-off exoskeletons of very large beetles. Yet each piece was so heavy and so solid that the management couldn't wrangle them out on the curb. Occasionally there'd be a yard sale and at one of those I bought a graceful gooseneck rocking chair for only twenty-five dollars. I was in graduate school then, and I couldn't afford to have it reupholstered, but I knew someday I would. I sat every night in that chair with a small glass of wine and a journal, beginning finally in my late twenties to rock and soothe and investigate my own soul, to decipher who I was alone, undefined by a partner. That rocker was a precious gift from an elder, even though we had never met.

I determined that Dad's room at the Landing would be a microcosm of all the homes I'd ever known him to inhabit. We winnowed the most precious of his possessions to fit his new space. On his walls, my sister and my friends and I hung his blacksmith painting; a snapshot of a vacation cottage rental we had visited so often as a young family; a photo of his barbershop chorus; a replica of an American Indian peace pipe he'd bought somewhere on his travels out West. I placed framed photographs of Mary Jane and his mother on the dresser and fashioned a mosaic of other family photographs next to his bed, to remind him of who he was, and to make sure the staff knew we were watching.

About this time, I began to watch over wild birds on coastal islands to the south, as a volunteer. Seabirds and shorebirds nest alone or in colonies, depending on their species, in shallow scrapes. Sandy open beaches, between the high tide line and dune grasses, are their homes, the only places they can nest and continue their kind. My first assignment was on a bit of sand only a few acres in size, a spoil island south of the Apalachicola bridge. There, I was to keep track of nesting activity by least terns, black skimmers, certain small plovers, or American oystercatchers.

Megan Lamb, my contact at the Apalachicola National Estuarine Research Reserve, had told me that this little island, unnatural as it was, had historically hosted a large congregation of brown pelicans, seven hundred nesting pairs. But after a large quantity of spoil was dredged from the river channel and heaped onto the island one winter, the pelicans abandoned the site and never returned. Another year, she told me, more than two hundred least terns and a handful of gull-billed terns nested on the fresh spoil. Megan couldn't say whether pelicans would return, or least terns—or neither. It could be a very exciting—or very boring—site to survey and protect, she said.

On my first trip to the island, before my kayak nudged against the hip of the sand, I looked first to see if any boaters might be trespassing. None today; that was good. What about aerial predators—fish crows, laughing gulls, and ospreys, the last of the winter eagles? An osprey perched on a post drying its wings, and two fish crows stood on the wrack line of the tide. In my new role as steward, I thought of those birds as thugs. All three startled away as I approached.

I soon learned why no other birders wanted to survey my new territory. Neither its shape, its smell, nor its vegetative composition appealed to the eye—or the nose. Along the shoreline, my feet sank into oozing mud where hard sand should be packed, were this a true beach. Still, the spoil island worked for some beach-nesting shorebirds because it was inaccessible to coyotes, cats, and raccoons and was unappealing to most humans.

It was so very hot. I rolled up the legs of my pants and slowly circled the island, with my spotting scope over my shoulder and my binoculars around my neck, keeping count of all the birds I saw. At either end of the land, south and north, wind drove shallow water against the sand, fussing the wavelets into white-tipped fringe. Birds stood about in good numbers, bathing and cooling their bodies. I felt at home when I saw the single white pelican among the flocks, and the broken-winged laughing gull. I knew them among the crowds of terns and sandpipers, from earlier visits to the site. Caspian, royal, and sandwich terns stood belly deep at the island's tips, flapping their wings and shunting water over their backs. It appeared as if the ends of the islands were trying to take flight or lift into the air, or

Shy and boldly patterned, American oystercatchers live and nest only on beaches and sandbars. Photo by David Moynahan.

were winged, with all those white and silver feathers in motion. But none of those species nested on the island; they only used it as a place for respite and feeding.

How would I find the solitary nests of the oystercatchers? They don't raise their young in colonies as least terns and brown pelicans do, so their scrapes in the sand are much harder to find.

The first clue was a turkey vulture skimming the sand, tilting on the heat of the barest updraft. Right on its tail, three American oystercatchers piped loudly, physically pushing the vulture out of the island's airspace. I'd never seen oystercatchers on the offense before, so I guessed there were chicks or eggs close by.

I crouched low and crept up the mound in the center of the island, to the edge of the topmost plateau. Through the white sand's shimmer, I spotted a pair of my birds, only seconds after they saw me. They scrambled to their feet, alert and worried. I knew that before I could settle my eye on the nest site, the birds would distract me away with quick wing beats. Before I even could guess where their treasure lay, the movement of their bodies would draw my eye to the left, tricking me from the nest. I withdrew, marking in my mind a post I might use to locate it with my optics. After I'd backed around the mound to a distance more acceptable to the parents, I set up my scope: Yes! Three eggs in the sand.

On a berm at the southern edge of the island, I noted another pair of extremely wary adult oystercatchers, and my eye began to perceive the birds' defensive ploys. They had slipped down across the broad spoil shoulder to watch me and wait out my intentions.

Their nest cradled only a single mottled egg. I squatted on the sand to wonder over it, but I didn't allow myself to touch the egg. No one was watching (no person, I mean), and I could have. Still, I curbed my reach, never even extended my arm. I think my desire to touch was connected to my human evolution, back to a time when eggs answered the need for protein, and when the practice of hunting birds' nests was solely linked to food.

I felt the anxiety of the pair who tended this nest, standing up the hill. If I were willing to invoke restraint, perhaps I could be almost an equal sensory partner. Our roles were so very different: I was the one who watched and wanted to know, and they were the objects I studied and counted and adored. Perhaps a relationship could be created if I agreed to curb my desire to be close, to back away, and to honor their subjectivity. It could be borne if I acknowledged their moral agency and the fact that they were engaged in the serious business of continuing their kind on the planet. I intuited the moment when I had nearly exhausted them with my insistence on being in their space. I felt their signal: *Go now!* they said.

My kayak scudded back to the ramp on the luck of a rising tide. The wind helped too, shoving into a line of black clouds building upriver. Glancing back, I watched a lone oystercatcher, an ember on the beach, keeper of a third nest I'd found. I knew the waypoints to return to her home: a single white post; an enormous log wedged into the sand; and a spread of white morning glories, blooming and perhaps scenting her long incubation with the company of their lovely orbs.

CHAPTER 9

Divine Counting

I felt proud: within the first three months of Dad's move to Tallahassee, his life had returned to good order. We'd distilled the physical goods of all his previous homes, and even his identities, into a small but pleasant space. I'd found a wonderful occupational therapist who had told me: "Your dad is too high functioning for a lockdown memory unit. Bob is still very able to rise to expectations." She confirmed my hope that assisted living could work out for him. We'd visited a dermatologist, an eldercare lawyer, an eye doctor, a podiatrist, the dentist. Two molars beyond repair had been excavated, and his teeth had been cleaned and polished.

"I like how my mouth feels now!" Dad slid his tongue over his teeth as we drove home from the dentist. He was ebullient, so much so that he raised the subject of the gracious manager of his previous nursing home.

"Hell, I'd marry her, if Bobbie would let me!" I let that pass and steered my car beneath the shade of an overhanging oak. With the windows rolled down, we mimicked the conditions of an outdoor picnic as best we could, unwrapping sandwiches from a favorite deli and listening to an interview of an Irish writer on public radio.

"We can do this, Dad." I smiled at him from the driver's seat of the car. I wanted to believe that as much as he did.

"Yes," said Dad. "But Sue, I've got too many sets of pants on." He plucked at the waist of his sweatpants.

"No, look," I said, walking my fingers through the layers of clothing around his torso. "These are your sweatpants and this is your underwear." I didn't mention the word *pullup* or *adult diaper*. "You've wearing just the right things. Perfection!"

"You mean perfection incarnate?" Dad chuckled. We dialed up Bobbie on my cell phone to report on lunch and the day.

"Girls, you have done an unbelievable job helping me get settled in Tallahassee," he exclaimed. "But then, I gave you something good to work with, didn't I?"

But what was next, now that we'd caught up his health care?

Several days later, I joined my father in the foyer of his facility. "I've been try-ing to remember the words to 'Old Dog Tray,'" he said. Sun streamed from the high, east-facing windows, lighting our faces. Eyes wide open, he warbled, not performing, not looking for anyone to join in. Just singing. "Old dog Tray's ever faithful / Grief cannot drive him away / He's gentle, he is kind; I'll never, never find / A better friend than old dog Tray."

"You girls used to like that one," he said.

Not many people were home at the facility. A bus had taken the spryest on an outing to the Junior Museum. One resident, a tall, white-faced woman named Mrs. Smith, sat at her assigned place at a table one full hour before lunch would be served. Two high school girls flanked her: they were shadowing the work of a caregiver for Career Day. They'd been assigned to keep Mrs. Smith company but instead giggled at each other behind their hands, unable to imagine how to interact with this woman who had lost her mind.

"Nurse. Nurse. Help me please." The old woman's voice was a reedy instru-ment. Her litany rarely varied. She knew she needed something, but what? The high school girls exchanged glances.

"Someone please help me. Can you help me? Please tell me." I'd seen how Mrs. Smith's thin repetitions annoyed her neighbors. Sometimes I'd see her seated in the sunroom next to one of the resident courting couples. When Ashley was out of earshot, the pair would yell at Mrs. Smith: "Stop that! You stop that right now!"

"Shut up!" Mrs. Smith would reply, her blue eyes snapping. A brief anger, a sense of injury would replace the pleading that looped in her brain like a necklace of prayer beads all her waking hours. The tall woman, once imposing, now wan-dered and wandered, lurching through the halls, looking for what she had lost, but it was her mind that was gone and it would not be found again.

I couldn't bear to think of Dad evolving into Mrs. Smith. And I really did not know how his disease process would unfold or what I could do to mitigate it. How I wanted order, and to taxonomize the process, and give the end of Dad's life some form and predictability. To know where we were: whether the beginning, middle, or end. I remembered how in the first year after Dad's diagnosis, I had studied the bible for families with dementia patients, *The Thirty-Six-Hour Day*. My dad had taught me well—now I was repeating his way of solving problems, no matter how intractable: Think, read, ask for help. Ask for help, think, read. I had tried to make Dad's illness fit into a timeline, and a stage (7c: Can no longer walk without assistance; 7e: Can no longer smile; etc.). I was looking for structure and certainty in a brain that was falling apart. Moreover, as I studied the disease online and in how-to books, underlining resources that might help and symptoms we might expect, I saw that I was studying Dad himself, objectifying my father and our relationship, just as I had the nesting oystercatchers.

So I called on our friend Dr. Ken Brummel-Smith. "Aging is tremendously variable," he'd once told me. "And much of that variability is under our own control."

We met with Ken in his spacious office.

"So good to meet you, Bob," said Ken. "Your daughter is a great friend of our family." He bent to grasp my father's hands in the wheelchair. And although he'd squeezed me into a quick hug, all of his focus was on my dad.

"So what brings you here today, Bob? How can I help you?" His voice and manner were steady and direct.

"Well, it seems that Alzheimer's disease is sitting on the sidelines, waiting to do bad things to me," said Dad, opening like a blossom under Ken's warm attention. He paused, not sure what to say next, and looked to me for support.

"We're hoping you can advise us," I said. "To tell you the truth, we wonder if you'll have a different interpretation of Dad's condition than we've heard so far." There it was on the table, our tenderest, biggest hope.

Ken scanned the papers I pushed across his desk: the diagnosis from Dad's neurologist in New Jersey, today's vital signs from Ken's nurse, a list of medications.

"Bob, I'd like to run you through a few assessments of my own, if that's okay," said Ken.

"Sure," said Dad, gripping the arms of the chair. He so wanted to please this doctor.

"Stand up for me with your walker and come on over to this chair beside my desk," Ken instructed. He kept up a steady chat while Dad moved slowly across the room. In silence, my father concentrated on his assigned task. I was on the edge of my seat. When had my father lost his ability to converse while walking, I wondered? Was this part of the test?

"Raise your eyebrows?" asked Ken. Dad did. "Stick out your tongue? Shrug your shoulders up toward your ears?" Those simple physical requests seemed reassuringly easy and Dad complied.

"Let's try a few questions. Bob, can you tell me today's date?"

"May 16," Dad's words tumbled out quick and strong.

"That's right, what year?"

"Nineteen . . . ?" Now my father fumbled to respond.

I found myself straining forward, wondering why knowing the date should matter. "Two thousand eight, two thousand eight, two thousand eight," I chanted silently to myself.

"I don't have any idea," admitted my father.

"Try this," Ken spoke kindly. "Can you spell *world*?"

"W-o-r-l-d," said Dad. I nearly clapped my hands.

"Now try that backward," asked Ken. But Dad shook his head no.

"Here's another," said Ken. "Subtract seven from one hundred, what do you get?"

"Ninety-three," said Dad.

"Good, keep counting backward by sevens."

Dad was stymied. "I'm a loser at this one," he murmured.

"No worries." The doctor was cheerful. "We are just trying to get a full picture of what's happening in your brain."

He passed Dad a pen and paper across his desk.

"Write me a sentence that describes how you feel, Bob. Anything at all."

Dad took up the pen, he who had written thousands of letters and reports in his lifetime. I peered over his shoulder as he worked. His cursive characters were small and crabbed, a line of miniature jagged peaks on the paper. Nothing intelligible to my eye.

"Can you read that out loud to me?" asked Ken. It was beginning to feel like torture in that office.

"Every so often I become frustrated," my father read off the page. Tears started in my eyes. I thought I saw a glimmer in Ken's, as well.

The next afternoon, I went to Dad's room to ready him for a follow up conference with Ken and my siblings. I found him deeply asleep in his armchair, without his glasses. I knew he'd had lunch: there were drops of something like brown gravy on his sky blue shirt.

We sat together, Ken Brummel-Smith, Dad, and I, with my sister Bobbie and brother, Doug, on speakerphone to confer about the previous day's exam.

"First of all, Bob, let me say that you're not the typical Alzheimer's patient," said Ken. "Most people don't respond to the medications that are given to enhance brain function, Aricept and Namenda. You are one of the lucky few."

"But is it true that I can't do anything to improve my ability to drive a car?" interjected Dad.

"Well, Bob, one thing I notice is that you have a lot of difficulty knowing where your body is in space," remarked Ken. "We call that magnetic apraxia. And I see that your left side is more affected than your right."

Dad nodded in agreement.

"So I don't recommend you driving, truthfully," said Ken. "What I hope you concentrate on, to slow the progress of this disease, is exercise. And mental stimulation. These are the things that will delay your brain's deterioration. You need to be walking a good deal more than you are now."

"Driving was a big part of my life," Dad sighed. "I'm not hearing anything very optimistic in this report so far."

Ken directed his voice to my siblings, who hadn't been present for yesterday's exam. "Your father tells me he sees himself living another six to eight years. A reasonable question is: should he be taking medicines that won't contribute to the quality of his life? I don't see anything really egregious on his list of medications," he explained. "But let's see if we can simplify what he's been taking. I'd like to set up Bob with a new primary care doctor in town, Dr. Mervin Wallace, and get his opinion."

"Next, let's talk about advanced care planning," said Ken. "There is medical technology that can keep your body alive, Bob, even after you can't do anything for yourself, including swallow food and water."

"I can't bring myself to think about that happening to me," said Dad.

Ken plunged ahead. "The brain function that controls swallowing eventually goes away. Tube feeding doesn't extend life and it carries risk of complications. And at that point in the disease, many patients need their arms restrained. I don't recommend that path."

Our father was speechless, and I was taking notes as fast as I could. We had to reckon with the facts: the chances that Dad could return to the fullness of the life he loved were zero. In fact, he would never return to any previous baseline. What Ken was telling us boiled down to this: don't confuse care with treatment.

In the days that followed, Dad reported nightmares in which he was forever trapped in his body, immobilized in his bed. Bobbie too dreamed of our family, all of us driving in a car with Dad at the wheel. That was her nightmare. My sleep had been marked by a happy vision of our family driving off into a western sunset as we so often had done in my childhood. Warm sunlight slanted on canyons and mountains. Both of our parents piloted our journey in the front seat of a big, old American car, driving into a beautiful evening sky. Which of our subconscious visions would come to pass?

When Christmas came round again, David flew home for the holidays and I was happy. Every night, we'd walk up to the garden and harvest the makings of our family's dinner. Bouquets of broccoli, spreading and gorgeous; Chinese greens and collards; lacinato and curly kale; parsley, cilantro, and the last of the peppers. All of these we stir-fried together, and it was as if my son had never left. I made big salads for lunch, composed of five kinds of garden lettuce, arils of pomegranate, and stems of Swiss chard, all Christmas red and green.

Near the end of his break, I sat cross-legged on the floor of David's room, helping him fill three cardboard boxes with goods to ship up to college. He packed a set of red headbands to wear during sweaty workouts in the gym, and I noticed how his shiny brown hair curled around his ears and down his neck. "I'm keeping it long until school is out, and then will cut it all off for summer," he said. He asked me to take a look at the seven-page application he'd been working on for a summer job with Outward Bound, but mostly I got my cues about how his life was going visually, not so much by talk. I watched him reach for a bottle of organic shampoo, triple bag and seal it with a twist tie. Just in case the shampoo leaked, he placed the eight-pound bag of super-nutty granola in a different box, with a white ultimate frisbee disc and his navy blue winter coat. I could see that he was taking care of his domestic life down to the sponges and coffee filters and vitamins. What I wouldn't see was the snowy Connecticut campus he'd be returning to, nor any of the ultimate frisbee games or practices he loved, nor his new girlfriend from California.

Terns, gulls, plovers, willets, and other shorebirds flock to rest, regroup, and care for their feathers. Photo by David Moynahan.

At the intersection of Saint Augustine Road and Blair Stone, stopped at a red light, David said: "I will miss Tallahassee. I'll have to make myself at home again up north in Connecticut."

It was the fifth of January, and we were headed east to the Amtrak station in Jacksonville, first through the smoke of a prescribed burn, then under a cloudy sky. We listened to David's music and I found myself trying to memorize every moment, the name of each group he enjoyed. Who is this person? What pleases him?

Meditation teacher Jon Kabat-Zinn says that it is helpful to look at our grown children as if we were seeing them for the first time, being with each one not as a newborn but as a new being. Any moment together, even on the telephone, is a new chance to be present, to build trust, to attune to them, to be sensitive, to be empathetic—to accept them as they are and to ponder their sovereignty.

David spoke: "I'm looking forward to making the name tags for the freshmen who will be on my hall this year. I've got a dinosaur theme in mind. Each new student a different dinosaur." David's love of dinosaurs as a small boy was something I had known firsthand. No one could take that from me, how I knew him. I smiled to myself.

As we pulled onto I-10, David looked over at me in the passenger seat and said, "Now, don't stress out on the big roads, Mom!"

"I won't if you don't drive over seventy-five!" I tried to mean what I said. But we were moving so fast into new territory. I wanted more time to molt this mother role and grow into what would come next.

It's difficult to advocate for something if you don't know how it is faring. If people or beings can't tell you with their voices how they are and what they truly need, how are we to understand how to help? No one outdid me in my passion and love for wild birds, but I was not among the most expert listers. Still, I knew that bird counting was important.

I took part in my first Christmas Bird Count, in South Carolina's Aiken State Park, in 1976. I remember garlands of American robins in the trees and cold approaching frostbite on my feet. My job, thirty-five years later, was exactly the same: to find and tally as many kinds of birds as possible in a single day on my assigned territory. It's supposed to be a census, but of birds, not people. On today's Christmas Bird Count—the 115th consecutive event—we were among seventy-two thousand citizen scientists observing the numbers of wintering wild birds. One of my territories extended from the junction of 30A and Cape San Blas Road, and Stump Hole, on the St. Joe Peninsula. My favorite stretch, and the most productive birdwise, was the beach.

It used to be—just a year or two ago—that you could not drive a vehicle all the way to the tip of Cape San Blas (that ever, ever changing point of sand). You had to carry your fishing poles and your beach gear either from parking places at Stump Hole or all the way from the houses near Money Bayou. Not too many people did, so wild birds thrived there, and you could usually find a great variety resting and rearranging their feathers.

But the protective barriers are gone now. With a cheap permit from Gulf County, area residents can motor the whole length of that beach.

As a result, I was a distracted Christmas bird counter. I should have been moving briskly, ticking off species and numbers of species, but I found myself obsessing about the impact of the cars and the people they ferry.

You've seen shorebirds standing around in groups on the beach and maybe thought they were loafing without particular purpose. But between forays to fish, shorebirds need time undisturbed to rest, regroup, and dry, reorder, and oil their feathers. They don't hide from us. They simply try to remain in the only places they can live, but we crowd them, we push them away. That's if we notice them at all.

Jeff and I set up my spotting scope a good distance away from the hundreds of birds resting at the spit and began to scan.

Royal tern, 110. Forster's tern, 97. Caspian tern, 2. Sandwich tern, 2.

I named off the birds and numbers of each kind out loud, so Jeff could record them in a small, waterproof notebook.

Black skimmer, 57. American oystercatcher, 3. Cormorant, 9. Brown pelican, 2.

I inherited my territories on Cape San Blas and St. Vincent from a petite, supremely businesslike birder named Barbara Stedman. In 2009, when I met Barbara, she'd already been keeping tabs along this stretch of north Florida coast for more than thirty years. While Barbara and thousands of other citizen scientists have been watching, their data show us that since 1967, absolute numbers of common birds have steeply declined. Some species have nosedived as much as 80 percent, including the northern bobwhite (quail). Many—like evening grosbeaks, meadowlarks, and several kinds of duck—have lost 50 to 70 percent of their population in just four decades. Those Christmas Bird Count data have been ominously corroborated in "Decline of the North American Avifauna," a September 2019 report in *Science* magazine. The authors point out that extinction begins with loss in abundance of individuals, which profoundly affects ecosystem function. Since 1970, the report finds that our continent has suffered population losses of more than 20 million terns and gulls, and more than 15 million sandpipers.

The losses, they slew me. Whenever I walked on a beach, my mind took refuge in counting—actually, first checking to see if there were enough birds to count. And always, I knew, that what I observed: say twelve red knots, eight ruddy turnstones, twenty-five sanderlings was but a fraction of what should be. Instead, I'd focus on what still lived, not what was lost.

A red Jeep came rolling down the sand, and several couples on foot moved toward us from the west.

"Jeff, quick, run between the birds and car tracks in the sand so the people will have to go around us," I asked, and he did. I pressed the legs of my scope more firmly into the beach. It looked like a stiff, mutant, three-legged spider. As if in a football game, we body-blocked for the birds.

Willet, 4. Dunlin, 41. Western sandpiper, 10. Ruddy turnstone, 5.

Most people driving or even walking the beach will respect a human's unspoken right to be where they will on the shore, and as I had guessed, these beach drivers circled around us to give us space.

Black-bellied plover, 1. Snowy plover, 7. Semi-palmated plover, 6. Piping plover, 3.

These same polite people may not have realized the nonnegotiable needs and extreme vulnerability of shorebirds. How would they respond if they knew that these very shorebird species had suffered such a rapid decline? And that our dogs and our cars are a large part of what's driving down their numbers?

As the beachgoers moved on, my concern for the birds relaxed. They were no longer numbers nor species threatened by human activity. They simply stopped me with their magnificent beauty. A royal tern chick, bowing to and begging from its parent, for food. Northern-breeding Bonaparte's gulls, with white-trimmed wings and scrappy dispositions. A black skimmer, so tired it might have fallen face down in the sand, except for its massive bill acting as a prop. I found myself suspended between the divinity of the birds and their utter vulnerability to human whims.

It was easier the next day, counting on remote and protected St. Vincent Island, a national wildlife refuge. I stood on the lip of West Pass, facing a warm wind and the rising sun; at my back, miles of salt marsh spread to the sky. I scuffed through the short grasses with my boots, hoping to herd sparrows toward the other birders in my party. Three different species of marsh sparrows piled up like Christmas tree ornaments in one small, skeletal shrub, long enough to clearly be identified. Using our bird apps and guides, we compared size and shape, nape and crown color, breast-belly contrast, and various streakings and stripes. I had studied hard for the sparrows, precount. Imagine the joy, then, of a chance to easily distinguish a seaside from a Nelson's from a saltmarsh sparrow. Heaven.

At Sheepshead Bayou, I trained my binoculars on a group of white wading birds standing at the water's edge. I needed to confirm that they were all snowy egrets before I added them to the day's growing list. My team members had turned their backs and were tallying bufflehead ducks, horned grebes, and common loons in the lagoon. They entirely missed the next miracle.

Magnified in my binoculars' field of view, a full-grown, soaking-wet otter emerged from the salt water and shouldered a path through the gathered egrets (nine snowy, one great). For all the world, it was as if the otter spoke to the birds: *Make way, make way. I've important business over in the marsh!* The egrets kerfuffled their wings and stepped out of the mammal's path. It humped briskly over the white sand and dropped into the juncus marsh, out of sight.

I admit I let out a little scream of excitement. I love this world so much. We have to name the things we will not relinquish. Counting is important—knowing how David was doing in school, knowing my dad's medical status, understanding how bird populations were trending, these things were important. But I suspected that numbers didn't change outcomes. For that we would need to dig into cause. The job I really wanted to sign up for was advocating for this world and the living things I cherished.

CHAPTER 10

Resistance (Only Leads to Suffering)

I did not want the life of the grown daughter who tended her invalid mother in the room next door to Dad's. Every single afternoon at five-thirty, the small woman would come bearing a fragrant paper sack from a fast food chain. She would wheel her mother to the dining room, cut her institutionally prepared dinner into manageable bites, and then unwrap a hamburger and french fries for herself. After they'd both eaten, the daughter would wheel her mother back to her room and gently close the door. The television they watched would talk through Dad's walls until nine o'clock, or later.

That wasn't the kind of arrangement I wanted. I craved long summer evenings walking the neighborhood with Jeff in the open air, watering our garden, cooking dinner from the vegetables we grew, sharing a beer on our own front porch. My father wanted that too, of course. But his immobility didn't allow for it.

Outside Dad's window, kudzu vines continued to erase the light. The growing season would last until first frost, around Christmas. I couldn't remember what that little woodland had looked like in spring. A friendly, very deaf little woman across the hall explained why she had moved out of my father's room before we took possession. "I hated the unnatural shade and how dark the room became every summer," she said.

"I really ought to take a chainsaw to that kudzu," I said to my dad. "Or pay someone to knock it back so the trees won't die." Dad didn't comment. The kudzu's regrowth felt so inevitable, I didn't take it on.

Another day. "Sue, I'm going to live to be 110," announced my father when I walked in his door. "But I'm kind of at wit's end. I'm not really sure what I should do with the small amount of time I've got left."

We had done the things I could think of, the tasks that Mary Jane had been too frail to accomplish. We'd been to the doctor, the ophthalmologist, the dentist, the oral surgeon, the gerontologist. But given the limitations of his disease, we couldn't do the things I'd imagined would help pass the time: play cards or watch long movies or adventure out in the car. He seemed muted, even less joyful to see me. His emotional register felt compressed.

And I felt like I was metering out my own life energy when I matched myself to his pace: pulling on his socks, solving staffing issues, walking alongside him to the bathroom, ever so languidly. I'd have to check my active body and mind at the door when I visited my father, and I could feel the pulse of my own purpose, my words, my desires, beating against his needs. We'd done this for four months, but how much time lay ahead? Dad's announced prospect of a long life ahead made me feel as if I'd quietly lose my mind.

I quartered a pale-skinned honeydew melon I had brought from the store. The bigger chunks I slid between Dad's forefinger and thumb so that he could ferry the fruit to his mouth. The smaller ones, the scraps, I hand fed him. I called my sister and Uncle Don, but neither answered the phone.

Dad worked at the Band-Aid on his elbow. He slapped his thigh. He rubbed circles on the fabric of his pants, a habitual gesture now. He slipped into a light doze in his chair.

Like an animal in a cage, I felt my soul compressed by the room's small dimensions. He surely did too. I knew my resistance to sitting in that room was only a fraction of how hard it was for him to be inside his own diminished state. I was beginning to despair of the daily visits, even though his joy—"Sue, you are here!"—would snap me back to the present and into the connection of our hearts. But much as I loved my father and despite a lifetime of connection, right now, for me, I didn't need to be with him more than two or three times a week.

There he was, lodged in a backwater of a sluggish creek of the end of his life. I had been alone all day writing and editing and I felt restless, and I didn't want to raft along at my dad's infinitesimally slow pace.

I opened and closed each drawer of Dad's dresser and desk, looking for something to organize. I pulled out his checkbook to settle his small accounts.

I thought about a recent dream in which I wheeled my father in his chair into the facility's elevator. We only wanted to go to the second or third floor, perhaps to the exercise class, but the elevator continued up, up, up. We couldn't get off. The numbers on the flashing digital indicator began to light up in confusing patterns. Finally, it stopped at the forty-seventh floor. But the elevator door was stuck. We couldn't go back down or get off. For how long could this continue?

Dad opened his eyes. "What are you doing, Sue?"

"Paying our bills," I replied.

"I'm going to take off my shoes now." Dad began to twitch and tug the legs of his gray sweatpants, hips to knees to ankles.

"Do you have to pee?"

"Yes," he grunted. It was no more fun for him than for me. I grabbed the plastic urinal and a cloth to mop any spills and buzzed the electric recliner all the way flat.

I helped him bend his knees, so he could lift his rump in a version of yogic bridge. He didn't comment or complain.

But his feet wobbled and drifted, and reflexively, he crossed his thin right leg over his left. He couldn't hold the posture, which was the only way I knew for sure I could help him pee without summoning an aide from the hall.

"Dad, can you lift your bottom, please, so I can help you down with your pants?" I readjusted his limbs.

He said yes. But he didn't raise his torso.

I touched his hip bone, thinking a physical cue might help. "Lift from here, Dad," I said.

We passed a full thirty minutes helping Dad get in position so that I could edge his pants over his hips, pull down his diaper, and position the pee bottle, only to discover the diaper already sodden, requiring that we somehow shimmy it out and replace it. It wasn't his usefulness I questioned, but my own. The work I was doing for him didn't feel like kindness or a gift, because I was so restless at my core. And certainly, it didn't feel like healing.

I was not writing, not organizing or advocating, and moreover Dad didn't even need to urinate after all. It felt as though we were moving ever so slightly in place, "as slow as molasses in January," as both my mother and father used to say.

Concentrate on why you are here, I'd tell myself. *Remember, this isn't your full-time job.* I was only with Dad four or five times a week, only a couple dozen hours of physical tending, plus shopping, phone calls, and appointments. But much as I loved him, I was bored.

Watching wild birds live out their purposes is my own life purpose.
Photo by Rob Diaz de Villegas.

I didn't feel bored when I sat with wild birds. I never did. My favorite thing was to find a resting clot of shorebirds and nestle into a dune to watch them go about their lives. On a recent day, the flock included dozens of Caspian terns intermingled with black skimmers. The sand where they stood was compacted by hundreds of tern and pelican toes. Royal terns were off to themselves. Pairs of laughing gulls mated; a south-borne wind lifted their feathers. Sanderlings and a few black-bellied plovers stepped through the crowd.

On the outskirts of the colony, I spied a single roving snowy plover chick. On long spindled legs, the chick investigated the beach all alone, its voice trilling a tiny stream of audible bubbles. He resembled a little marshmallow Easter chick, except covered with gray and buff down, instead of yellow sugar. No tail, no feathers at all, a soft white cowl on the back of his neck. I watched him stop to scratch his chin with a naked black foot.

I couldn't tell if that tiny chick alerted when the skimmers rose and circled, when their light nasal background honking shifted to a louder, more urgent *waah waah waah*. What and how did the chick know to fear? It could not know, as I did, that it had come highly endangered into a highly endangered world.

The parent plover knew. It flew back from the water's edge to drive away a sanderling that had ventured too close to its young one; I hadn't thought of a sanderling as a threat. If I were able to visit the birds only once in a great while, I wouldn't feel the rhythm of their lives, nor witness the coast processing through its intricate seasonal and geological changes. I needed to be with them, to see for myself what was at stake.

As the adult plover skirmished with the sanderling, its chick took refuge under a small green dune plant. When the adult returned, the chick beelined to its parent and burrowed into the feathers of its breast. The newly hatched plover chick came into its world possessed of a bold life force. Plover chick, plover parent, and every other creature out there on that beach by swelling Gulf waters do nothing but fully live their purpose. I wanted to rise up every morning and do the same.

Away ran the plovers, speeding over the sand. I sensed that the parent was rushing the chick past a laughing gull standing close by, which seemed smart. Even I knew the laughing gull meant danger. I was left alone with the little bird's tracks. The creature carried so little weight. Its prints were whispers in the sand. I felt deeply happy to experience a short window into a plover's life and to sit quietly near the rare birds I loved so much. To witness, be present. This is my sacred profession: to be with the birds and then tell their stories.

Sometimes on a slow summer evening when I was a child, my father would become a bird. He would lean back in his chair and push away from the long kitchen table in our rented beach cottage. He would tighten the muscles of his belly and thighs, straighten his knees and lift his legs. He'd press his feet close together and point his toes. He would throw out his arms as if they were wings and pretend to glide.

Through tightly pursed lips, he'd whistle, "Wheeeee!" He'd ask, "Guess what I am?" We children would whoop and scream at the unexpected oddness of the moment and urge him on, the way he was playing, mimicking the cry and float of the laughing gull.

It was a solo act. Dad never suggested we join in, never expected anything at all from the eight or nine of us at dinner. "It just came over me," maybe he'd say that much. You could take it as a joke. You could take it as a tribute. He never explained. He'd pick up his beer and resume his banter with our Uncle Frank. We kids would clear the table for cards.

Outside in the dark salt night, on once wide and sufficient beaches, the real birds—the plovers, the terns, the oystercatchers—would be raising their chicks.

But we didn't know about that. Way back then, the laughing gull was the only seabird I knew by name and habit. We should have known better and more, given the many weeks we spent at the Jersey shore, and on North Carolina's Hatteras Island. For us, the shore and sea birds were decorative, and the beaches (their essential habitats), our playground. We loved the wild birds, wouldn't have wanted to imagine the world without them, but we had no idea what they required to prosper, nor how our runaway culture was affecting their lives.

With my shoulder, I shoved open the Landing's front door. From my right hand swung a red net bag of single-serving cheeses. In the crook of the other arm, I juggled an enormous box of adult diapers. Just inside the lobby I was happy to see Gretchen, my good friend, ferrying supplies to her own dad, Woody, who had recently, against his will, moved into the Landing. We dropped our packages and fiercely hugged.

Gretchen was a beautiful woman: long-limbed and graceful, a great blue heron with glossy black hair. She was a yoga teacher, a mother of three, a schoolteacher, and one of the most adventurous of my friends. We had spent many days with our young children kayaking, swimming, and camping on rivers and Gulf beaches. She was a dancer too, and her father's aging enforced a terrible inertia on her own body that I recognized in myself.

Yet the prospect of spending time with my old friend and our fathers made me glad. I imagined it might be like the slow times we had shared nursing and playing with our children, cooking meals. But Gretchen was teaching full-time, so most of her visits were in the evening. I looked in on Woody whenever I walked past his room. Any hour of day, he was likely to be sleeping on his single bed, his head slanted awkwardly on the pillow, his left arm dangling almost to the floor. Even my own father didn't sleep as much as Woody. We all agreed he seemed depressed.

Woody much preferred the many months he had lived with Gretchen in her tiny house, but it was too small to share indefinitely, and his needs for human contact were too great to fasten on only one person, this daughter, no matter how generous her heart. She felt crowded out of her own space. Woody's hearing was limited, so he filled her house with Fox News from nine in the morning until nine at night, loud. Gretchen's preference, left to herself, would have been quiet music, or even better, pure silence.

Now, when I'd spot Gretchen out on the patio with Woody, sitting cross-legged and graceful on the rattan porch furniture, we'd widen our eyes or roll them at one another. In my friend's body, I saw the same feeling of entrapment that I felt, as we sat our respective vigils with the kind men who had raised us. In fact, none of the four of us could freely move: Gretchen and I were not ready to be so slowed and stilled in our bodies. But our fathers had no choice. They were incarcerated within the collapsing neural structures they'd taken a lifetime to construct, and there seemed to be no way out.

Time passed. The winter holidays approached, and I sat beside my father with wrapping paper and ribbon, putting together gifts and cards for the facility's caregivers. My friend Rebecca was visiting, telling Dad about her trip north by train, and my brother was in town too. Dad felt the currents of activity flowing around him in the room and understood that little of it had to do, in that moment, with him. He thrust himself into the flow of flying words and the back-and-forth, summoning his best effort at communicating his needs, his state of being.

"I want to go . . ." said Dad.

A visit with more than one person, or a visit when the full attention was not on him, would create a profound unease in my father. While everyone else still charged about their lives, here he sat, bound to the body and brain he was born with but which no longer allowed him autonomy.

He mentioned wanting to visit a long green park or go to bed. Each spoken destination was accompanied by physical impetus forward with his body, as if to stand and walk, a movement toward getting up and leaving.

"Do you want to go to another chair, Dad?" I offered what I could.

"No!" He was antsy.

"I'm sorry we can't go outside, it's too cold. Do you have to go to the bathroom, would you like me to help you pee?"

Yes. That seemed like it would help.

"Now, Sue, clip my fingernails, please." I was glad he enjoyed the small ways I groomed him. I gave up on my chores, put away the tape and scissors and scraps of paper, realizing how I had contributed to the contrary energies and impulses in the room by not being fully present, by multitasking with the brightly wrapped tiny jars of honey, and the checks, and the conversations that he could not follow.

"Sue, I need to . . ." Dad said urgently. I moved toward him.

"What do you need, Dad? A hug?" And he held his arms out for my embrace.

"If you could travel anywhere in the world, where would you go, Dad?" I was still thinking I needed to fill up the space with talking or dreaming or hope.

He didn't reply but reached for the remote control of his chair, which for the most part he'd lost the ability to operate. He pressed the arrow labeled UP, raising his chair to its highest position, EJECT. If he'd had any momentum at all, he'd have shot facedown onto the floor. Again I noticed the impulse to rise and leave an untenable situation, one where he could not succeed in being a full participant and knew that fact to be true.

"What's up, Dad? What are you doing?" I shuffled his walker in front of the chair to catch his fall. I could sense the intention to walk, to stand, to move about freely in his body. I could feel the lift of his arms into the fence of the walker and the slightest press of his thighs and his chest, up.

"Where do you want to go, Dad?" I asked.

"Out to the side of the road," he said. "I just want to go," he said.

Finally he fell deeply asleep in his chair. His mouth slackened and his breathing grew deep and full as he let go into a place where he could be unconscious, for a time.

A few days later, a caregiver named Melanie grabbed my sleeve as I walked down the corridor to Dad's room.

"Now, I know you don't mind me getting all personal with you, Sue." Her words poured out in a rush, compressing the last four frustrating hours into the length of time it took us to walk the hall to Dad's room. Melanie had strong features, dark brown eyes, and intensely curly hair. I'd seen her smoking outside the kitchen door in the evening between clients, and I'd seen her in animated conversation with a very tall man on the front porch. His aspect was shaky and wild. If that was her husband, I thought, her life must be scary. But Melanie wanted to please me and I appreciated that. Not all of the aides did.

"I just told your father, 'Sue is driving up, and she's not going to be happy finding you here with your jogging pants down around your ankles.' But he refused to pull up his pants, and when I tried to help him pee in the bottle, we stood there five minutes and he never actually did it," said the aide.

Apparently, Dad had fought fire with fire. When Melanie gave up and left the room, "Nurse, nurse!" he had yelled. This dynamic repeated all afternoon, she told me. She'd try to work with him, he'd refuse. She'd leave the room, he'd holler for help.

In his room, Dad lay in the big blue overstuffed recliner, trying to thread his leather belt through his shorts, which were down around his knees. A gray sweatshirt was sprawled on the floor. He clung to my warm hand with his cool one. Almost always, Dad's face would light when he first saw me, and he'd tell me how glad he was that I'd come. But this time he didn't smile.

"Dad, what's going on?" I asked.

His voice was hoarse and gravely. "I'm trying to clean up this mess around here." His shirt hung open, unbuttoned.

"Do you have a sore throat, Dad? Do you need some water?"

"No, I was shouting."

I drew a chair up close to his, fact-finding, even though my first impulse was to yell at somebody myself. I knew Melanie and the other aides were hovering outside in the hall, waiting to see how I'd deal with the situation.

"What made you so mad?"

"Them shouting at me," he said. "It was disappointing to have them all ganged up on me." He began to fidget the white buttons on his shirt, pulling the two halves of his garment together across his chest.

I knew it would take a long patience to sort out what had happened, so we began with just the first layer, more about how he felt.

"Sue," he said. "If you were stepping into an organization, that would be one thing, but if you were stepping into an abyss . . ."

"Sounds like life feels out of your control, kind of chaotic," I said. He swung his eyes to meet mine. How does one step out of dementia, once the disease has invaded your brain? Given that there is no cure? I listened to my father state his experience, and I knew he could not. But, I thought, surely if the dementia is an economic or political system, surely then we had more of a choice?

"Have you had dinner yet, Dad?" I'd passed the other residents gathered in the dining hall. Given his state of undress, I knew he hadn't yet eaten. Food was always a comfort in our family.

He didn't want the beef steak and mashed potatoes the cook had set aside for him on a white china plate covered with plastic wrap. But raisin bran and milk sounded good. I set him up with a bowl of cereal on the blond wood TV table, and while he spooned the food into his mouth, I sat beside him and listened.

"I have to be more tolerant of the ways of these girls," he said.

"You know, Dad, their job is to help you. But you need to do your part, as well. Do you think you could apologize to Melanie for fighting with her?"

"That's implausible," grumbled my father.

"Can I help you with a shower, Dad?" I asked. He shook his head no. When the Landing caregivers offered to help him bathe, he would cross his arms over his chest and refuse. Usually, he would allow me to groom him, but not reliably anyone on the staff.

"Then let's do a shave and a little wash up right here in the chair?" I offered. In his bathroom, I filled a pink plastic bin with sudsy warm water, then loped out to my car to fetch his toenail clippers. If I left them in the room, invariably, they'd disappear.

After Dad finished his cereal, I soaked his hands, left, then right, in the warm water, trimmed and cleaned his fingernails.

"I wonder why I have dirt under my nails," he said, watching me dig under his thumbnail. "Since going outside doesn't thrill me anymore." He was beginning to relax.

"It could be food," I said, "Or maybe bits of skin from your scalp?" He'd developed a habit of raking the tender skin on top of his head vigorously, and "as often as I can!" Scratching off the scabs he'd created on his head seemed to be a way to displace stress.

"If only I could find your sister Martha," said Dad. Martha's troubles worried my father, deeply concerned all of us. "If I could, I'd bring her down here and move her in with me, take care of her."

I emptied the soapy water and drew a fresh batch. I snugged a towel around his neck. I knew all the ways he scrunched up his cheeks, how he'd shift his chin and jaw left, and then right, pulling his skin tight to get the closest possible shave. As a child, I'd watched him tend to his own grooming so many mornings.

"David has enrolled for organic chemistry, physics, and neurobiology, Dad!" I told him. "What a smart grandson I have," he said. "And where's your husband?" Jeff was off playing tennis, I said. The muscles of my father's face were starting to relax.

I washed his hair. Shampooed, the short silver hairs stood up glinting and shiny, and his scalp was pink, cleaned of scabs and scruff.

"Once, during World War II, I was in the back of a convoy truck guarding some German prisoners," he said. "It was so scary trying to figure out how closely I should guard them with my gun." I'd never heard this story before. It seemed to come out of the blue, but then he confided: "My balance has been so bad lately. I am really scared of falling."

The facility's aides experienced Dad as recalcitrant and resistant, but underneath all that mad, he was scared and confused. I'd still have to deal with them. Either apologize, make up on his behalf. Or scold them. And/or report what had happened to Ashley.

I squatted on the floor and peeled back the Velcro fasteners of his shoes, wriggled off his socks. He didn't complain when I submerged his feet in the warm soapy water, but neither did he register pleasure.

Just before bedtime, Christine, practical, taciturn nurse Christine, rattled her cart of nighttime medicines into Dad's room.

"Time for your pills, Bob!" she said. "Can you stand up for me?"

At first, even using the electric tilt function of his chair, we could not get him on his feet. He could not find a place of balance. It was as if the complex musculature most of us so take for granted, all of those long, core muscles, were collapsing in random directions. No, he could not stand. I knew what the aides were up against.

Finally, by leaning all my weight into his walker, we were able to half-coax, half-lift him to his feet. We edged a urine-soaked pullup down his legs. An angry red triangle slashed across his thighs and buttocks.

"His skin is irritated from sitting too long in urine," said the nurse. We washed his poor old flaccid buttocks with soap and water, and then Christine massaged zinc oxide into the skin.

I wondered if Dad's recalcitrance this week could be attributed to the painful butt rash. I knew I was grasping to make sense of a disease that didn't. But I also knew one thing: in the presence of people he knew and trusted, he did best.

"I've got to sit down, girls," said Dad. "I can't stand any longer." One at a time, I lifted his feet off the carpet and eased on a clean pullup and soft flannel pajama bottoms. Back in his big blue chair, he leaned his head against the ribbed corduroy, and waved a hand at the television screen.

"Could you . . . ?"

"Turn on the TV?" I asked.

Yes, he said, closing his eyes. I dialed the sound way down low, because I knew he wanted me to have something to watch so I'd take my attention off of him. He was too tired to interact anymore.

I looked at the clock on his bedside stand. The process of mending his day had taken nearly two hours. *I can do this*, I thought, as I dumped the soapy dishpan full of water down the drain. *I know how to get these basic things of comfort done.* Perhaps my resistance was even a good thing, I thought—how it delivered me to a deeper level of attending.

I watched him as he fell into sleep. Recently, Dad had told me I spent too little time on my own work in the world, too much time worrying about and caring for him, so I'd made plans to travel to the wildlife and climate change conference the next day in Orlando. I'd paid the registration and reserved a nonrefundable room. Dad wanted me to go. I wanted to go. I needed to hear what the latest research was showing for the book I was writing about our coast. Yet all the care I'd just offered, the sorting through of my father's needs, all that would be of no use to him tomorrow. I made a vow to hire more consistent, reliable help.

CHAPTER 11

Beulah and the Notebooks

Here was the one true fact: Dad's illness, seven years into it, had left him able to do exactly nothing for himself. Not turn on the sink or open the refrigerator or read a book. Not operate the telephone, take a shower, or brush his teeth, not without help. He could not reliably move his own body through space. More than once I had found my father clinging to the rail I had paid to have installed in his bathroom, unable to lower on to the toilet or turn back into the room. He—we—were completely dependent on the attention of the Landing's staff.

One Sunday afternoon, I arrived fifteen minutes after the facility's shift change. There were very few cars in the visitors lot. When I walked in the door I heard piano music. About fifteen folks were parked in the living room in their wheelchairs, but not my dad—surprising, because he loved live performance.

I noted that Christine was on duty in the nurses' station—she was always good with my dad. I passed Miss Annie and Miss Abby sitting in armchairs in the sunroom, dozing. Everything and everyone in place, so far.

But rounding the corner, I heard a dreadful rattle, like an angry kingfisher circling a creek, a loud, mechanical "NO NO NO NO NO NO," underscored by softer, sharp yelps. I sprinted down the long hall, tracking the noise. Lucy and Melanie and fear and anger and sweat filled my father's space. Dad's face was puffy and damp; he roared. The two women, dressed in kelly green aprons, were enforcing a diaper change.

But Dad had Lucy gripped by the forearm with both of his hands. "NO NO NO NO NO," he was shouting, holding her back from his body. Grip and bellow: that was all he could manage. I was horrified and they knew it and Lucy tried to cover it over with assurances ("Sue, it is shift change, we are required to check his diaper now."). Melanie stood her ground and glowered. I dropped my purse on the floor. "Stop it," I ordered. "Stop what you are doing right now."

"I'm here, Dad, you are okay now," I ducked in close and spoke into his ear, over and over again, trying to soothe. But he wasn't able to respond, not even to express his outrage and despair, so battle spent was he. "Let's just get him in his chair," I said to Lucy, and she helped me ease him into a more comfortable position. Then the two women picked up the sodden diaper from the floor and fled. I'd lost my ability to make nice with them, to smile and connect. I felt my father's sense of violation. But I also knew how hard he was to assist when he was afraid.

I crouched on the floor beside my father's chair, stroking his arm and his forehead, crooning. Blood reddened my fingertips. Now I understood the source of his frequent elbow lacerations. I had just seen for myself how hard he fought when he felt attacked, abrading his skin against the rough blue corduroy of his recliner. My anger was vast; I felt it rise. *They are not to force him anymore*, I thought to myself. Dad lay still, eyes closed, breathing.

After a bit, I fetched a fresh peach from his counter, peeled its furry skin with a table knife, and cut it into a small bowl. It had been brought to me from the mountains of North Carolina and its flesh was abundantly ripe. I knew it would comfort his throat, which was spent from all the shouting.

Lucy returned in tears: I knew she cared very much about doing her job well. In the evenings after the management went home, Lucy often did extra vacuuming and made sure napkins were folded and tableware in place for the next meal, while Melanie and others watched, arms crossed over their chests, or scrolled through their phones.

When Dad relaxed, I jogged back to the nurses' station, rapped on the locked glass pane.

"Christine, they are not to force him anymore," I cried. I looked in her eyes, pleading. "I swear, Christine, if I have to move him, even to my own little house, I will!" Christine, who was so devoted to her job and without whom Dad would fall between every crack, heard me out.

The nurse's brush-cut hair and flat demeanor belied her utter commitment to caring for these old people. She said—I remember it so clearly—she said, "Sue, your dad would lose so much ground if he were moved." She held my gaze, her brown eyes level and full of truth. "He would have to start all over again, and that wouldn't be easy at all, for either of you."

I took another breath and I thought about others here, the weekend nurse, Danny, whom I'd seen lift my father in his arms like a child, when he could not stand to get in bed. And nurse Paula, whom I genuinely loved, who always hugged me like a sister. And Patrick, the cook; he deserved a book of commendations all his own.

While we talked, a resident named Miss Abby approached the door. Abby moved like a robot, never turned her neck, never ever smiled, her mouth a permanent horizontal, her face an expressionless mask, holding, I thought, a great terror in place.

"Go listen to Ms. Vera's music," said Christine. "Go sit down, Miss Abby."

"I already did. But I've heard we are scheduled to die." Her voice held a south Georgia lilt. "*Dah*" she said. "I've heard we are scheduled to *dah*."

"You must be scared," I said. Miss Abby turned her neck and shoulders and eyes all of a piece, and said, yes, she was, and now she was ready to latch onto me for comfort.

"I need a minute more to talk with Ms. Sue," said Christine, turning Abby by the shoulders and easing her back out the door. Christine then told me how she'd brought her own father home to die, eight years ago. He was in his nineties, and even though she had to stay up with him straight through four days and four nights as well, it was all worth it because when he came into her kitchen on the first day and sat in a chair at the table and her little dog jumped into his lap, "It's so good to be home" he said, and that moment carried Christine through the next ninety-six sleepless hours, the stretch of time it took him to complete his dying.

Dad wanted to come live with us so much. Often he'd say, "Sue, I want to go to your house to live."

Or he might say: "Today, I started out walking to your house."

"I know that's what you wish you could do, Sue," said Christine. "But my dad wasn't like your dad. You couldn't do that for him. He's not dying, and he's too hard to physically handle." Still, we both knew how limited his quality of life had been lately and how great his suffering, especially last week with two episodes of painfully impacted bowels. It wasn't acceptable for him to suffer any level of abuse on top of the disabilities brought on by his failing body.

I was very upset about my father and equally desperate about my own work. How could I protect him completely and still get my own writing done?

It was Bermuda-born Beulah—the first of the outside help I hired—who began to bring order into my life and advocacy into Dad's. Her hair was cut into a squared-off Afro, pure white, and her eyes were as deep as coffee. She carried a big black bag, which contained a French language workbook, crossword puzzles, snacks, and knitting. She'd leave me a brief note every night, listing supplies needed for Dad's room and any issues of concern. I'd always write back my thank-yous.

But Beulah preferred to talk things through after her five-hour shifts with my father. Surely I owed her that, didn't I? "I prepare myself every day for what is to come in the evenings with Mr. Bob," she had told me. She wasn't a young woman, nearly seventy, in fact.

Midmorning, her call would come. If I was home, I would dump a load of clean clothes on our bed. I'd slip headphones over my ears and fold and listen.

"Hi Sue, good morning, Beulah here, touching base."

"Beulah, hello, so good to hear your voice." I shook out a green T-shirt and folded it in half on the quilt.

"Your father and I, we had a wonderful night last night. We watched the Travel Channel, a program about the country of Laos. And we really enjoyed it. He, especially. And I know you'll be happy to hear that Mr. Bob spoke to his brother on the phone; they had a wonderful conversation."

I was very glad to hear that; contact was important to both my dad and his brother, and Beulah made sure it happened every night.

Beulah continued. "And I tried to get him to clean his teeth, but he was confused. He definitely did not want the electric toothbrush. So I got the manual one and he still couldn't do it himself."

I murmured into the phone, stacking our T-shirts in two piles on the bed.

"So I said to your father, 'Well, let me just try to do it a little bit' . . . and girl, do you know he let me clean his teeth! And he rinsed his mouth, and then he went to bed."

I truly was grateful for her kind pacing and told her so. I separated out Jeff's thick black socks from my white ones.

"Then I gathered up two soiled outfits and a dirty towel that had some cereal spilled on it. I went down to the laundry and washed them. Lucy was there."

"How was Lucy with you, Beulah?" I asked.

"She's not happy with me being in the laundry room. But I stayed cool, calm, and collected. I'm just sort of keeping my eye on her." Beulah laughed. She knew she was my eyes and ears, and she was committed to bringing me every detail. So far, we'd been on the phone more than twenty-five minutes. I told Beulah I needed to get back to work.

"Okay, Sue, I'll talk to you later. Have a blessed day. Bye-bye."

I'd hired Beulah to replace me so I could redirect attention to my work. After a time, I asked if she would record her reports in a notebook, so I could keep up more easily with her observations of my father's evenings.

The reports from Beulah lengthened into several pages a night. She worried that the Landing staff would read our communications. I couldn't imagine anyone else wanting or willing to read the excruciating minutia of Dad's evenings, but still we hid them in a manila envelope on the top shelf of Dad's kitchen cabinet. Beulah's script was precise and elegant, and her attention to my father's needs was absolute.

Dad couldn't report on how his nights had gone, the good or the bad of them, not with any coherence. I hadn't realized how much I needed Beulah for that until she had filled in the lines for me.

She'd call when things were tough. One Sunday morning, Jeff and I paddled far out on the Aucilla River. I'd left my phone in the car. Hours later, guilt twanged my heart when I heard her steady voice and the content of her voicemail.

"Hi Sue. Good morning, it's Beulah, touching base as usual. Your father had sort of—I'd call it an unproductive night. I found him somewhat withdrawn. We watched *The Lawrence Welk Show*, and afterward he wouldn't get up from his easy chair to go to bed for a long time."

She drew out the word "long" for emphasis.

"So I didn't press him. I just sat patiently until finally somewhere about ten minutes after nine, mind you, he made a motion to get up and I got him out of the chair and settled in bed nicely.

"And I said to him, do you want me to read? And he said, 'No, I'm too tired. I wouldn't be able to concentrate.'

"Then your father said: 'I think this disease is getting to me.' So I told him, that's the reason why we just take it one day at a time. And then we had our prayer as usual, and he went to sleep.

"Sue, we really need to get more pullups and underpads and he's requested prunes to eat. Just thought I'd let you know. Take care. Have a blessed day. Bye-bye."

Before my father became ill, he documented his own life in letters exchanged several times a week with his brother, my uncle Don. Dad kept yellow legal pads nearby at all times, and high-quality ballpoint pens, whether at home or traveling. The two men reported to each other on trees planted, home projects constructed, the activities of grown children, books and ideas, and increasingly on doctors' visits.

But my father couldn't write letters anymore and he hadn't been able to read a book for some years. "Sue, I can't get any action out of my eye man," he had complained. But in a small examining room, the ophthalmologist had explained that because of the disease, Dad's eyes and his brain could no longer communicate with one another, not through written language. It was a terrible loss.

I'd scan Beulah's log entries for clues: an upturn in Dad's strength, or a good meal ingested, or a timely bowel movement. She wrote and I read for the same reason: to see if we couldn't bring structure to the disease that was toying with and killing my father's brain. Dementia is a chaotic place to live, filled with emotional tension and challenge.

I noticed that the spiral bound notebooks containing Beulah's reports were piling up far more quickly than my own words in my journals or on the pages of the book I was writing. My hope had been that leaving the constraints and assignments of my agency position would free up my pen and my time and return my attention to other ways of perception and writing. But I was still struggling with my roles. Mother and stepmother to three sons grown out and away. Daughter of an aging father needing a good deal of my help. And lover of a planet increasingly under assault.

As much as I wanted to console my father, I wanted to speak for the Earth. To do that, I needed to dedicate myself to writing. To have something worth saying, I needed to spend more time—days and weeks and months—at the coast. I needed to place myself into direct experience and intimacy with the birds, not simply digest and reword what I'd been taught or could glean online. As a child and a young adult, I was taught to be faithful to the church, a traditional education, my parent's conservative politics, state agency organizational charts, even the language of science. The wild birds, and my love for them and fear for their fate, pulled me loose of those constructs.

One day, knowing Dad was safe in Beulah's care, I drove down to the coast to a little Gulf access called Wakulla Beach. I took off my shoes and waded across an ankle-deep tidal inlet, making my way toward a cluster of birds I wanted to observe. Sun chased over the clear water's surface. Up ahead, in the salt creek, something bobbled in the water. I eased closer, not knowing if it was animal or plant. The object was shaped like an old-fashioned garden dibble, avocado green, thin, longitudinally salt-wrinkled. It was a mangrove seed. And it was tracing a message in the sandy bottom.

What was it writing? I wanted to know. I watched it sway in the mild tide. It drag-floated at the exact depth to activate its writing tip, the growing cusp of the seed. It was as if a small aquatic animal tailed through the shallows, leaving its track. Wading behind, I followed its inscription on the floor of the creek. If I hadn't caught the mangrove seed in the act, I'd never have understood the source of the story in the sand.

It drew mountains. It drew curves. Retreating and advancing, it followed the water, telling the story of the tide as it scribed a path in the sand. Staying with it, I could see that its response to the water's pull was extraordinarily precise. A pen that free and that sensitive could allow me to pay attention to all kinds of knowing.

My voice could no longer be denied. I was flooded with spontaneous prayer: *May my passage through life and my writing be as pure as the Earth's own pen. Please,* I entreated, *may it be so.*

And so began the writing of *Coming to Pass: Florida's Coastal Islands in a Gulf of Change.* When I returned to my house, I inscribed a fat black journal with a single word—COAST—and affixed images of oystercatchers and sand dunes to make it beautiful.

I didn't know what this book would become, at first. "At the core of every piece of work is the question," wrote David James Duncan. "You may not answer it, but you are always moving toward it. Your ability to articulate a question is what will make for a good writing. It'll be a trail marker."

Welcome evidence of endangered red wolves on St. Vincent National Wildlife Refuge. Photo by David Moynahan.

I began to articulate the things I wanted to learn:

What is the unique nature of this coast, geological, biological, human/cultural?

How were the islands formed, and how are they changing?

When I was born in the 1950s, there were but 300 ppm carbon dioxide in Earth's atmosphere. Now it contains an increasingly catastrophic 410 ppm. How can I address that in a way that others can hear?

Was there ever a time when people lived inside the shape of this landscape, in reciprocity, not simply on top of it? What would that be like?

I copied those questions and many more onto the first pages of my coast journal, which I kept in the fashion of a commonplace book. I began to record interviews with scientists, jot notes on the tides, sketch snowy plovers, copy passages from the myriads of experts whom we really ought to pay attention to, like Orrin Pilkey and Cornelia Dean, and from poets and sages like Henry Beston, John Hay, and Leslie Marmon Silko.

Over time, I allowed my own body and my own senses to listen to what the coast might want to be said directly. I offered myself as a conduit. More and more space in the journal became devoted to the voices of the birds and the sand and the seeds. I fixed my words, my tracks, in my notebooks, just as rare shorebirds lay their footprints in the sand, and side by side with the paw prints of St. Vincent's she-wolf and her pup on that island. I would learn to meander, to sniff, to observe, to explore, just like those wolves on the beach. In a relaxed, curious state, with steady attention, I could learn to be present. I would learn to move so that wild animals would feel safe in my presence. Taken together, maybe our tracks would say: We were here, and we found it beautiful beyond all imagining, and worth every effort to preserve and protect.

I didn't know I'd be left with the notebooks kept by all of my dad's caregivers, over the next four years, beginning with Beulah. They still occupy a corner in our storage shed, a stack three feet thick. I couldn't throw them away, for it was the notes of our personal staff of caregivers that allowed me back into my own writing.

"Being good is not sufficient for these times," said the great healer, writer, and wise woman Deena Metzger. "What you are called to do is really, really bear witness."

CHAPTER 12

Then We Hired Jill

On the porch of the Landing, men and women gathered in oversized green rockers to enjoy the end of the day.

Tall, bald Roscoe pushed through the front door and headed toward a potted hibiscus on the sidewalk. "Where's your babe magnet?" asked another resident, referring to Roscoe's dog, Tigger, who often occupied the laps of resident ladies.

Roscoe didn't answer until he had pinched a single crimson blossom and tucked it behind his ear.

"In Hawaii, this means you are available," he grinned, aiming his remark at no one in particular. Except I noticed a pink flush bloom on the cheeks of one quiet old woman across the porch.

"That Roscoe is cutting in on my territory," Dad grumbled in my ear as the banter continued. I wondered if the same woman had caught my own father's eye.

"There's a lot of drama around here, Dad," I said.

"It's slow moving," he replied.

I dialed up my sister Bobbie on my cell, and as was often the case, Dad turned the conversation to the perennial problem of romance.

The Landing's recreation therapist, red-haired and curvy, stopped to greet us on her way home. Dad's smile opened, broad as a wedge of cantaloupe. The young woman rested a hand on his shoulder.

"Don't forget, Bob," she said. "Sittercise is tomorrow at ten in the morning. I want you to come and join us." Dad tiptoed the fingers of his left hand up her forearm. Gently, she disengaged, and blew him a kiss. We watched the young woman walk to her car.

"How kind she is," I said. "You should to go to her exercise class, Dad."

"She sounds great," said Bobbie, through the speaker on the phone.

Dad (right) and his younger brother, Don, shared a deep, lifelong bond.

"She could stand to lose a few pounds," our father said.

"Dad!" I chided. "That is not your business!"

"Dad, have you ever had a relationship with a woman who was just a friend?" Bobbie was exasperated.

"You can't divorce the two, friendship and love," said Dad.

"There you go," said Bobbie. "You've put your finger right on the problem!"

"How old would you say she is?" asked Dad, ignoring my sister's counsel.

"About twenty-eight, I guess."

"God Almighty!" yelped my dad. Even he knew a woman in her twenties was too young for him.

My sister and I chuckled. Our father was not amused.

"Why are you two being so selfish?" said Dad. "I'm allowed to fall in love."

"She is my daughter's age, Dad," said Bobbie. "Pursuing her is out of the question."

Later in the evening, I tilted back in a black ladderback chair next to my father's bed, my feet propped on his bed frame. The voice channeled through the speakerphone on the nightstand was Uncle Don, my father's little brother, seventy-seven years old to Dad's eighty-two.

"What have you got on your calendar this week, Rob?"

"I've got to make contact with my three paramours, Don," said Dad. "You know I've got these various love interests, and I don't want to make a mistake. For me, our age differences seem to fade away. But I don't think the objectives of my interest are so sure about that."

Uncle Don replied, "Maybe you should just cool it for a while, take it easy?" His voice carried not a scrap of judgment.

"I can't last forever, Don," said Dad. He lay in bed on his back, eyes shut, hands folded over his chest. The corners of his mouth curved in a foxy grin, which made me smile in turn.

"And I admire that dedication," replied my uncle, who had been married to only one woman—my aunt Carol—compared to my father's five wives. "But it sounds exhausting to me. It reminds me of the last half mile to Camp Yaw Paw—all uphill!"

I grabbed the chance to divert my father from his fantasies.

"Tell me about Camp Yaw Paw, you guys?"

"Sue, it was a great place to go for the weekend when we were teenagers, our Boy Scout troop's Adirondack shelter," Uncle Don said. "There were six bunks in a row behind long sashes of glass that protected the whole front of the cabin from the weather. But you had to hike three miles uphill from the paved road trail to get there. And after you'd trudged the first couple miles with your pack and all your supplies for the weekend, that last half mile seemed to take a mighty long time."

"Don, I don't know if I'm capable of cooling it," mused my dad.

I found my father's optimism inconsistent with his situation. If he weren't flat on his back in an assisted living facility. If we hadn't so recently buried his fifth beloved wife. If I hadn't just helped him into his plaid cotton pajamas, dark colors, mismatched top and bottom. If he weren't wearing a pullup under his pants. But we were learning never to underestimate our father.

It wasn't easy to find caregivers who could work with Dad's special set of needs. His mind was reasonably good, sometimes, but his body was very weak. And he himself wanted companionship and respect, not just physical help.

One evening, I ran into Jill, a midwife and a nutritional counselor, in the market. She was part of our larger circle of friends, free-spirited and easy to talk with, and Jeff and I both liked her a lot.

"Would you be interested in some part-time caregiving work?" I asked. We stood between shelves of canned beans and soups, where I was searching for my dad's between-meal snacks. Jill named her hourly rate.

"Come and meet my father, and let's talk."

Jill cut a lively wake through the Landing's male residents when she arrived to interview for our job. She wore tight velvet pants tucked into black boots and a lacy, low-cut, cream-colored blouse. Her lipstick was brilliant crimson. Looking back, I wonder if Dad thought I'd bought him a girlfriend. Years later, after his death, Jill told me he was the best boyfriend she'd ever had.

The urge to procreate, to physically mate and bond, is not restricted to the human species. One of the most intimate, life-affirming acts I've ever witnessed is the courting ritual of the larger tern species.

On the first of May, I walked along Dog Island under a sky purple with storm. The wind blew grit and rain against my skin. I was so happy to be out among the many sea- and shorebirds. Given the weather, I knew I would not have to share the beach with any other humans.

It was a black-and-white shorebird day on the front beach: it seemed that every bird was sharply drawn and freshly feathered, ready to breed. There were snowy and black-bellied plovers, two avocets, dunlins, and sanderlings. I couldn't remember ever seeing so many ruddy turnstones, especially in their fine spring feathers. A clutch of black skimmers had fallen asleep, with their beaky faces propping them up on the sand. They lounged like fat cigars, their crimson bills long red embers, burning.

At the last tip of the land, three kinds of terns—slim, graceful seabirds—royal and Sandwich and least—negotiated their courtships.

I dropped to my knees behind a small dune, moving carefully to keep my rain pants from crinkling. I didn't want to disturb the pair of Sandwich terns standing closest to me, side-by-side, on the beach. The male elongated his neck and drooped his gray wings, like shutters. The female spoke to her mate, insistent, cheeping. *It's time, it's time*, she seemed to say. *I'm ready, my eggs are ready! Now!*

He obliged, skipping up onto her back. Double-decker, the two faced into the wind. The male planted his feet into her feathers, and she pressed her own breast into the sand. She leaned her head against his sternum, craning her neck and pointing her bill to the sky. The pair gazed eye to eye, and then the male twisted his underparts to join with hers. He beat his wings softly, balancing his body aloft, intensely chattering. A minute passed, then two. Steady rain pelted me and the mating terns equally. Then she shrugged him head over heels, and again they stood side-by-side on the beach, facing the sea, rousing, then smoothing their feathers.

A few weeks after Jill began work, Dad and I sat in the waiting room of a gerontologist recommended by family friend Ken Brummel-Smith. I'd wheeled Dad close to a big window, so we could enjoy the sun. I opened a lined notebook I'd labeled "Dad's Healthcare."

"Let's make a list of the physical issues you'd like the doctor to address, so we don't forget anything," I said.

"For starters, if I really do get married, it'd be fun!" He tilted his head, eyeballing my expression, hoping I'd go along with his dream. "But I had a vasectomy thirty years ago. I'd like to see if it could be reversed. That's number one on my list."

My own list for the doctor did not include a vasectomy, so I tried to insert a little perspective.

"Who was your favorite of your wives?" I asked.

"The one I'm planning to marry next!" he grinned. He was eighty-four years old, but he giggled like a boy.

"There are probably some questions you should ask if you're getting married," he mused, looking out the window at the pine trees lining the parking lot.

"Like what?" I stuck my pen back in my purse.

"Number one: Do you snore? Two: Do you treat money cavalierly? And then there is housekeeping. I don't think I'd be happy living in a complete shambles." I had to agree.

"And then, there is this: Who were those two guys in Jill's garage anyway?"

I pondered that remark, really no more odd than the rest of the conversation.

A nurse slid open the glass door separating us from the doctor's examining rooms.

"Mr. Isleib?" she called. I undid the brake and wheeled my father through wide double doors.

I steered the conversation with the new doctor toward my concerns: diabetes, mobility, and constipation, and asked him to take a look at Dad's scalp.

Dr. Wallace ran his fingers through Dad's fine white hair, noting the scabs: "Neurodermatitis," he said, and prescribed a soothing cream.

Could we take Dad off one of the three medications prescribed by former faraway doctors for high blood pressure, I asked. "Dr. Brummel-Smith suggested we stop the blood pressure medication since his numbers are fine." Dr. Wallace agreed.

Only one set of body parts remained unaddressed: the genitals. I asked Dr. Wallace to check out locations where we'd identified irritation and reddening skin.

"Shall I leave the room so the doctor can examine you in private?" I began to edge past Dad's wheelchair toward the door.

"Do you want your daughter to step out?" asked the doctor.

"No," said Dad. So I sat. The doctor performed a quick exam, prescribed zinc oxide and an antifungal. *Now it's coming*, I thought to myself. *Dad is going to talk about sex.*

Dad's illness had forced the end of a lifelong modesty. I'd never seen his lower torso unclothed until he was eighty-two years old; now, as primary caretaker, I saw it all. Wiped and diapered. Inspected every inch for rashes and bedsores.

Actually, I did see my father naked one single time, when I was fifteen years old.

"Time for supper, Dad!" I had called, knocking on his closed bedroom door. "Mom says we are eating outside on the patio tonight." I turned the knob to make sure he had heard me.

My unclothed father was so startled and disturbed, he executed a spontaneous *jeté*—a leap I'd only seen before in ballet class—and of an elevation I wouldn't have thought him capable. He held his striped boxer shorts in one hand. His privates dangled between his thighs. Deep red shame flooded his face.

"S-s-sorry, Dad!" I said, slamming shut the door. We never talked about that incident. That's how circumspect he had always been.

Dr. Wallace had peeled off his exam gloves and stood at the sink washing his hands.

"I would like to get my vasectomy reversed," said my father.

The doctor was ready to sign off on Dad's chart and move to the next patient, but I give him full credit for what he did next. He pivoted back to us, lowered his body onto a round stool, graceful as a dancer, and heard my father out.

My father was a very old white man crumpled in a lightweight traveling wheelchair.

Dr. Wallace was young and agile, born and raised in Dominica. His skin was very, very black and his teeth were white as pure salt crystal.

"Why?" asked the doctor. "Are you thinking of having more children?"

"No," Dad replied. "But things aren't working very well down there. I'd like to be more functional in that department."

"Are you in a relationship or planning to get married?"

"Yes," said my dad. I shouldn't have been surprised, but I was.

"Well," said the doctor. "We may have to separate issues here. Reversing a vasectomy is one thing. I'd have to refer you to a urologist to see if that's even possible. How long have you been experiencing erectile dysfunction?"

"About fifteen years," said Dad.

"I suggest an alternate plan," said Dr. Wallace. "Why don't we focus on seeing where you go with this relationship before we get into surgical options? Then we can come back to this issue."

The doctor did not crack the tiniest smile throughout the whole of that surreal conversation. He was completely respectful of my father but more than a little relieved, I suspect, to return the problem to me.

A few days later, I paced alongside my father, escorting him to his room. Dad bent over his walker, moving one very slow step at a time, heading for his room. We used to have a physical therapist who loved Dad and could get away with saying things like "Bob, don't crouch over like Mr. Magoo! Stand up straight!" And he would, for her. But I didn't say that now.

We were only halfway down the hall, as far as Mrs. Smith's old room, when he stopped. While I waited for him to continue, I noticed that the nameplate had been pulled off Mrs. Smith's door. She had died a week ago, and her room would soon be occupied by someone new. Dad scoured his scalp with his fingernails, the way he did when he had a problem he couldn't solve. I knew that his own mortality was not on his mind. It was a question, really, about Jill. She had taken several days off of work, and I knew he missed her.

"Are you worried about Jill?" I asked. "Are you worried that your relationship with her is off somehow?"

"Yes," he said, trying to articulate why. Once we settled ourselves in Dad's room, I dialed up Jill. Mercifully, she picked up her phone.

Dad straightened tall in his high-back wheelchair when he heard her voice through the speakerphone. We stared out the window together, watched the light shift into evening.

"Don't worry, Bob, I'm still committed for the long haul," said Jill. She had driven her daughter to the train station in Jacksonville, that was why she'd been gone.

Dad brightened and brightened. He cuddled the phone containing her voice against his cheek. A smile crept over his face. His eyes were half-closed, picturing her face in his mind. He took a big leap, his biggest leap, offered up his heart.

"Well, then, Jill," he said, "can you handle a ring?" He spoke happily, beseechingly, confidently. "How about a diamond the size of a lozenge?"

In that moment I could see exactly how his face must have looked when he proposed to my own mother, tendering his best offer, a golden promise. It was this moment of offer and likely acceptance that was peak for him.

Given a "yes," he could know himself claimed, coupled, and safe.

Jill smiled, and Dad was satisfied.

After we ended the conversation, I gave my father a quick shampoo and clipped his nails. I noticed he wasn't wearing socks, so I slipped off his shoes and pulled a clean stretchy pair over his feet. The socks still bore his name, labeled in his dead wife Mary Jane's script: "Bob Isleib."

"Sue, do you really think I can pull it off?" His voice was full of excitement.

"Pull off what, Dad?"

"Managing Jill! Can I still handle a woman that lively?" He was greatly cheered at the thought. One at a time, I levered his shoes back onto his feet.

Atul Gawande in *Being Mortal* wrote, "Our most cruel failure in how we treat the sick and the aged, is the failure to recognize that they have priorities beyond merely being safe, and living longer. The chance to shape one's story is essential to sustaining meaning in life." What passed between my father and Jill was born of deep and genuine feeling, despite vast gullies of difference in age and ability, despite the fact that Jill had a primary relationship with a man her own age.

In my journal, I wrote:

Birds bind with silver, not with gold. And to my eye, their marital arrangements are far less complicated than those of humans. I floated in my kayak on the azure Gulf near a place where least terns nest on the shore. I chose a distance that would not disturb a pair of courting birds standing on the shining sand. The female shirred her wings, fluttering soft like a dove, the very image of receptivity. The male stood before her. His bill pinched a living fish the size of a soup spoon. As he moved his head side to side to tempt his mate, the last angling of the sun struck the body of the fish. My breath caught: it appeared that the tern offered elemental silver to his mate. She accepted his nourishment, both actual and ritual. Fish dies into bird, bird fertilizes an egg, and life proceeds through the intricate lovemaking of terns and the sacrifice of small fish. The terns bind one to another, vowing to protect and feed a pair of chicks until they can arrow the waters from the bow of the air and confidently obtain food for themselves.

Such lovemaking, that fragile and that powerful, is the source of rare eggs this pair will brood on the sand. Such lovemaking is what continues life on this planet. We humans make our desires the measure of all things, and that has left little room for wild birds. Like the sick and the aged, like the poor and the very young, they are profoundly marginalized in our present-day world.

CHAPTER 13

The Many Forms of Grace

"When it's your turn to live here, when you are too old to care for yourself, who will you be like?" I addressed a playful question to Ashley on a slow Friday afternoon in the Landing's dining room. Our eyes traveled over the faces of all the elderly residents around us. "Miss Annie Ray!" she said, indicating the tiny old woman sitting at the table next to my father. "No question about it." "Why?" I asked. "She's always ready to be happy," Ashley replied.

Miss Annie's eyes were magnified by huge, pink-framed glasses smudged with her own fingerprints. She had a quick smile and loved to hold your hand.

Ashley passed Miss Annie a book of carpet samples. The Landing staff was planning a redecoration. "Which is your favorite?" asked Ashley. "What color should we pick for the living room floor?"

"Goodness gracious," Miss Annie exclaimed. "Gracious me!" She ran the tips of her fingers over each vivid square, one after another after another.

"Red!" she said, no hesitation. She brushed the square of carpet dyed crimson, and through her eyes, all of us shared in the simple amazement of red.

"Miss Annie, I'm going to get some milk for my dad from the kitchen," I said. "May I bring you something?"

"Yes," she said.

She clasped the heavy glass goblet to her lips. "Gracious!" she said. "Apple juice!" Her sips were sacramental, awe, the taste in her mouth.

Grace was easier to find in the daylight hours, for Dad had become an unreliable narrator of his own life, and if anything, less able physically, than ever before. I now paid someone to be with him from 8:00 a.m. until 8:00 p.m. every evening of the week. In shifts, five capable women operated like a hive of bees in that room, attending one immobile larva in his chair. You could say: what a waste of resources for one old man. Some people did say that. And besides, some people said, no matter how much help you hire or provide, you cannot protect your father from the course of his disease.

But I thought the network of care in Dad's room was transforming each one of us into something we may not have imagined and it had everything to do with love. Infused into this room were Jill and her warm vitality; Beulah's prayers; Shirley's great humor and energy; Gail's serious attention to duty; Esmine's tender and vigilant heart. Dad would appear to be at the center of this world, but many lives were being lived in this room. Also orbiting Dad's dense planet were hospice staff and other caregivers and the voices of Dad's faraway children and brother. I was in the web too, but I was not central, or even, perhaps, essential. I solved problems, praised, supported, wrote checks and schedules, brought a thread of constancy to my father's care, but my efforts were nothing without the rest.

Still there were the long stretches of the nights, from eight in the evening, when our paid caregivers helped him to bed, until eight in morning, when another of our own trusted staff returned. Other families whispered rumors of rough treatment at night. How was I to know?

Very, very early one morning, I was awakened by a nightmare in which my father was calling my name and pleading for help. I slipped out of bed, pulled on my clothes, and drove the two miles to the Landing. The facility's massive front door was locked, so I sneaked through a low hedge of boxwood shrubbery and let myself in through the kitchen. I hoped I wouldn't startle the staff.

No one moved about the silent facility, but Dad's door was open, sending a triangle of light into the hall. Inside, a young woman was making up his bed. She heard the door creak and turned to face me. Her name tag read "Iclene." She smiled at me, somehow unsurprised.

"His bed was soaking wet so I got him up and changed him," she said. "We check on them all night long."

Dad was dressed in daytime clothes, resting in the recliner, awake and still.

Iclene bundled up the soiled sheets and left the room.

I crouched beside Dad's chair, took his hand. "Iclene seems very kind," I said.

"Sue, see if there's some food we could eat together for breakfast," he said. His demeanor was very calm.

In the kitchen I found Iclene. I'd been wanting to meet her. I'd been told she sang to Dad by the gas log fire in the living room, in the middle of the night sometimes when he couldn't sleep.

While I rustled around for wheat bread to make toast, I asked her about herself. Iclene was twenty-four years old, a student of nursing at Tallahassee Community College, an employee here at the Landing on the 11:00 p.m. to 7:00 a.m. shift, and a member of Bethel AME Missionary Church on Tennessee Street. "You'll find me there every Wednesday and Sunday night," she said. She wore black plastic glasses, was very tall, and kept eye contact as we talked.

And she stood very still like a graceful forest animal, her hands folded together in front of her diaphragm, as if she were at that moment—perhaps in all moments—in prayer. And it was true.

"I pray for strength all the time," she said. "I ask Him for strength. He gives me what I need."

The bread rattled in the toaster. Iclene reached in the industrial refrigerator for butter.

"He got me this job," she said, referring up beyond the ceiling, to her God. "So I know He'll give me the strength to do it." Ashley had told me Iclene worked the eleven to seven shift four nights a week and attended classes in the daytime.

"Do you go to church, do you pray?" she asked.

What I told her: "I pray with a circle of women," referring to my Womanspirit group. But my eyes skittered to the toast I buttered, away from her gaze. I didn't share her faith, certainly not the structure of her religion, and I did not attend an organized church, as I had done as a child.

What I didn't tell her: that my personal theology requires that I pray directly to and for the Earth. For me there is no greater authority. "Align me, O Earth, with your purposes," that was the litany of each day for me. I didn't tell Iclene that, all of my adult life, I'd found divinity in remote woodlands and shorelines. In the cycling of day and night, the moon, the seasons, and the responding constellations of wild birds, this is where I reentered the silence and located my prayer.

When I returned to Dad with his toast, he had fallen asleep. I set the plate of food on a bedside table and slipped out the door. In the parking lot, a rim of light in the east caught me by surprise. "Wheep," called a great crested flycatcher from high in the pines. Once home, I stretched out on my bed, taking in all that I had seen. I dropped into peace. No more fear. Only peace. Struggle had left me, at least for the moment. And then I began the rest of my day.

For each of his four children, Dad had a lifelong agenda, had zeroed in on at least one issue he hoped we'd resolve before he died. About my youngest sister, he worried: would she ever be financially secure? My brother: why didn't he stay in touch better, invite him to visit more frequently? My sister Bobbie: maybe she was the exception, pretty close to perfect. But regarding me, his oldest child, "The only thing I care about," he would say periodically, until he could no longer string the words together, "is that you're still a Christian." My father used to gather himself up and get purposeful regarding my relationship to God. "I've been thinking about something," he would say, "about grace." He sent me books and articles, asked me to go to church with him whenever I visited. But my spiritual support came from a meditation practice, and through circles of women, and from time in natural places—and was little informed by patriarchal religious doctrines. The spiritual offering of the Landing was tricky for both us.

Three evangelical Christians from a local church had ministered every Sunday afternoon for the three years Dad had lived there so far. Attending their services was the easiest way to get him to a place of worship.

A tall, fearsome woman led the invocation dressed in tight suede boots, black hose, a calf-length black skirt with a kick pleat, and a golden jacket that matched her hair. Then she moved to the piano bench for the hymn sing, the residents' favorite part of the service. A second woman, short and round, wore wire-rimmed glasses over pretty blue eyes; she walked inside the perimeter of wheelchairs, conducting vigorously with her left arm, while her colleague pummeled the keys. The third, a man, searched room to room for folks who might want to come to church but didn't know it was time.

The first hymn was about being ready for heaven, or getting prepared if we weren't, by accepting that Jesus was tortured and died on the cross for our salvation. I paged through the large-print hymnal, looking for softer, more accepting canticles like the Presbyterian hymns I had grown up on. Most of these songs were Baptist, just as stern as the evangelicals themselves. There was little mention of love or kindness in the lyrics, and nothing of the Earth, nor the gift of our embodiment.

I squirmed in my chair, slid my eyes away from the preacher, and fussed with a button on Dad's sleeve.

"Dad, can you think of a hymn you'd like me to request?" I whispered. That's how it worked here. You hollered out your preferences and the pianist accommodated as many as she could. But my father's body had descended into a C curl in his wheelchair, and he didn't respond.

A new woman had moved into the room next door. The previous resident, a wispy, white-haired, Germanic woman, would melt into tears at any act of kindness, or even warm eye contact, during her last months wandering these halls. Now we had Miss Juanita as a neighbor. She set up a sewing machine by her door and we often heard it whir. I noticed in the church circle that a pair of tubes fed oxygen into her nostrils and that her face was pasty white. Still, Miss Juanita thumped her hymnal against her knee in time with the beat of the piano. Her eyes were closed, and I could tell she was invested in content as much as I would be if Brenda were playing "For the Beauty of the Earth," or better yet, a song by Becky Reardon, any one of her songs. As it was, I practiced reading the alto line and tried to disregard the words. Dad revived and chimed in with his pretty baritone.

We sat through a brief, fiery sermon. I tried for just the right balance of eye contact to establish my polite attention but cut off any energetic connection that might lead me to confess my sins or feel the urge to become born again. Then it was time for personal prayer. The three evangelicals moved around the circle of residents, and when it was our turn, I suddenly longed for them to pray for my son David, who had been diagnosed with a chronic illness. Dad wanted that too. We wanted a God who could heal him. The lay preacher reached out for my hand and Dad's, and I grasped my father's left palm. All around the room, I could hear the murmur of the prayer-team members sitting with the other old folks, one by one addressing their failing bodies, their wayward children, their lonely or fearful hearts.

"Let us invoke the power of God to heal Bob's grandson, David, to drive all disease from his body," prayed the leader. Her eyes were closed and she tightened her grip on our hands before she continued. I truly felt she believed her version of God could cure my son, and in that moment, I did too.

"There is a Bible verse for David, Isaiah 53:4–5," she continued. "'Surely he hath borne our griefs, and carried our sorrows: yet we did esteem him stricken, smitten of God, and afflicted. But he was wounded for our transgressions, he was bruised for our iniquities: the chastisement of our peace was upon him; and with his stripes we are healed.'"

Again, I was repelled. Why did David's healing depend on the torture of Jesus two thousand years ago? Nevertheless, the urgent need to believe filling that room overlapped precisely with my yearning for my own beloved son to be well. Tears flooded my cheeks. I connected with my heart. I gave over my worry to the evangelists' God with gratitude, without judgment, against all odds. I was no longer an observer, a companion to my father, but fully present in this room filled with grace and the surely dying.

The door was open to Kathryn Crown's room. I had passed by hundreds of times on my way to Dad's but never had knocked or entered. But this night I thought maybe Kathryn Crown needed help. The white-haired woman's hands were cupped over her blue housedress against her chest. She sat erect in her chair, gathered up as if every part of her strained to support her heart and her lungs, as if all the rest of her body, each part with its own rightful needs, was willing itself into stillness—brain, no needs; liver, no needs; intestines, nothing. It seemed as if every organ in her body was ceding its oxygenated power to the heart and lungs, in the interest of blood bringing breath. Her head rolled right to left, then back. She moaned. I worried that she might be dying.

"Mrs. Crown, Mrs. Crown, I'll go get help!" Without waiting for an answer, I ran to fetch the on-duty nurse.

Later, when I left Dad's room for the night, I looked in again on Mrs. Crown. She was alone, but she had oxygen now, two long clear proboscises connected under her nostrils to a tube leading to a sturdy green tank. I sat beside her, touched her hand.

She found a scrap of her voice and patted my hand. "You feel sympathy for me, don't you, dear? Who are you?"

"My dad is Bob Isleib. He lives at the end of your hall."

More liquid than air occupied her lungs. Her breathing was the sound of an espresso machine. The tank forced air through the mucus. I shuddered at the fight between air and water, how those elements contended.

We sat quietly. Her fingers were cool in mine. The retired music professor across the hall yelped like a lonesome puppy, all broken down and barking in the night.

White pelicans winter in the shallow marshes and bays of the northern Gulf of Mexico.
Photo by David Moynahan.

Mrs. Crown was kind. "The professor isn't lucid tonight." She had barely enough breath for words. If I were her, it would intensify my own fears, to listen to the man's cries.

I offered to bring her ice or some water. She nodded. I didn't know which, so I filled one glass with just ice, another with water and ice. One for myself, too. She wanted me to sip along with her, to share a moment of normalcy. But her breath was a louder presence than our conversation. She could barely hold the glass to her mouth. I found a stack of straws by the sink and slipped one from its paper sleeve. I kept thinking all those little things might help.

When the nurse returned, I left. I heard Mrs. Crown say she hoped I'd come back.

Sitting with a person I'd never met near the end of her life seemed to me like trying to piece together the life of a rare mollusk from its empty shell, on the sand.

Mrs. Kathryn Crown, who were you and what mattered and still matters? I thought of how much—and how little—I had learned about this woman on this late Thursday night. She once lived on Live Oak Plantation Road. She belonged to a quilting circle. All her friends had gone to bed early tonight, so she was alone when her symptoms worsened. On a little wooden table next to her chair sat a skein of wool—baby pastels—the kind that changes color every few inches, marbling like an infant-inspired sunrise. I fingered the metallic rose crochet hook on her nightstand and asked her what she was making.

"Little blankets for the premature babies in the hospital," she said. "They need so much help keeping warm."

As I drove to my home through the dark night, I thought about Kathryn Crown, how steady and kind she was, living out her purpose until all her breath was gone. Mrs. Crown knew I needed practice with the dying.

Finally a little break for me and for Jeff. It was a quiet orange sunset, and we sat on the deck of a rental house at Indian Pass, a stretch of days ahead of us. The tide was so far gone, so far out, I wondered if it would ever return. But small broad combers were beginning to angle back into the pass, urging against the sandy shore. The moon-pressed Gulf would have its way, I knew.

"Are those white pelicans on the point?" asked Jeff. We'd never seen them loafing there with their smaller brown cousins, and it was late in the season besides. But there they were: magnificent huge knobs of snowy white, across the water on the refuge. Binoculars brought them close: seven white pelicans standing at the water's edge, adjusting their feathers.

I'd seen them arrive in long, determined squadrons from the west in the late winter, often over the St. Marks Refuge; and I'd seen them rise on warm spring air, describing the spiraling currents. But never here, and never at nightfall.

Birds never spend the night on the western point of St. Vincent Island: it is avidly patrolled by predatory raccoons and wild hogs. So it didn't surprise me an hour later when the seven gathered up into the air, fell into a lopsided V, and flew directly over our heads. They flapped so close and low we could hear their great wings creaking.

The routes and nesting grounds of the white pelican have been extensively mapped, but we know nothing of the intimacy of their journey, how it is decided who will fly with whom, and how far to travel in a day—and why these seven stopped at Indian Pass for just this hour. I felt so grateful for the confluence of time and space that allowed us to watch them and sit with and beneath them in awe. In a matter of days, these seven would arrive at their summer grounds, in Utah or northern Canada, and commit to the urgencies of nest building and egg laying. They will not remember us wishing them well on their leave-taking of the Gulf of Mexico. But perhaps our prayers for their safe passage might in some way sustain them.

"If we do not see nature as somehow carrying the divinity," wrote Jungian scholar James Hollis, "we will continue to abuse it."

The white pelicans' flyover assured me that where I stood was on their map and reminded me that we shared a common sacred Earth: our true home and our church.

"This is grace," I said to Jeff. "This is a grace we can trust."

CHAPTER 14

Violence

I sat beside my father while he rested, stroking his left palm and fingers. It wasn't a big hand. With age, the transparent skin had softened and shed its calluses. Dark blue veins forked the length of his fingers. Those fingers had held mine as a baby and a girl, had done all the work of a man's long lifetime, had carried a gun in World War II, had hauled coal to the cellar furnace in our home, had buried three of his wives. Now my father's hands were simply vulnerable, sentient, and frail. Lost in reverie, I turned his hand over and gave it a little pat of thanks.

But wait, what was this? There was a seeping cut below his third knuckle. Configured in the shape of a crescent moon, the wound corresponded in size with my own fingernail. Someone assigned to his care had pressed her nail into Dad's papery flesh until she drew blood, punishing him for resisting, forcing him to comply. With what, I could only guess.

We had encountered similar situations in the New Jersey facilities, before I was fully in charge of my father's care.

On a visit north, Dad had told me that "a mean bitch" had pushed him down roughly, in the face, at night.

"What did you do, Dad?" I asked. "Did you report her?"

"I told her to quit it, that she had crossed the line," Dad said.

When I was a very young child, my dad took me by the hand and led me out into the night, my baby sister Bobbie perched astride his shoulders. We three stepped into our backyard, leaving the safety of our house behind us. The moon shone on our swing set, but it wasn't familiar or inviting in the dark. "Look, girls, do you see the stars?" We lifted our faces to the sky. My father had brought us outside just before bedtime, because I had told him I was afraid of wild foxes coming to get

My dad and me, 1953. Photo by Janet Isleib.

us in the night. He was demonstrating that I was secure in the world and that he would always keep us safe.

Now it was my father who needed my protection, something I could not seem to guarantee. I could not promise that he could trust the night.

"Where did you get this cut, Dad?" I asked, turning his hand in my own.

He winced with pain. He answered indirectly.

"Sue, I need you to write a letter to the Johnsons for me," said my dad. I pulled a pad of paper from my father's desk and scribed a sentence of introduction.

"Dear Bob and Sally: Dad has been thinking about you a great deal and wants to write you a letter."

I looked up at Dad, ready for his dictation.

"Bob and Sally, I think it's time for me to kill myself," he said. His words came all in a rush. He looked out the window, not at me. "I can't see why I'm always being beaten on. They are much bigger than I am. I'm strictly a has-been. I just hope I keep consciousness until . . ." His voice trailed away. I wrote down every word he said, but I knew I wouldn't be sending it to his friends.

Dad sat quietly, still staring out the window. "Doesn't your husband have a rifle, Sue? I need some way to defend myself around here."

I sat in the chair, holding my impotent pen. The same anger and sense of injustice that had gripped his body now ruled mine.

I jogged to the main office and flung open the manager's door, interrupting a meeting between Ashley and her assistant. Breathing hard, I insisted they look at the picture I'd snapped of Dad's wound with my phone. Ashley's response was sympathetic, but she shook her head. "We can't rush to judgment, Sue, we need to hear the caregiver's perspective. Because Bob cannot fully report his experience, due to his dementia, we can't be certain of what might have happened when no one else was present."

"Ashley, there is no denying this situation." My body trembled as if I were my violated father. "How are you going to make this stop right now? Tell me how."

She leafed through the caregivers' schedules. I knew she was wondering herself who had been on Dad's hall last night. Her assistant proposed that Dad might need drugs to make him more compliant with the staff. "Risperdal works well for many of our folks, at night, to keep them calm."

I was outraged. "Look, you two," I said. "One, you are not going to drug him. And two, you may only allow caregivers into his room that can absolutely be trusted not to hurt him." I told them I'd be requesting who I wanted by name, and who would not be, never be, acceptable. I knew I was bluffing.

This wasn't the first time my dad experienced the consequences of living with women stretched beyond their ability to cope.

"Oh, she was tough," Dad had told me, many years before, about his mother. "Charles she called my father, and Donald, my brother, and me—Robert. Not Robbie or Don or Charlie—or dear.

" 'So, so, so,' she'd chant under her breath if her round of chores was falling into place and she could see the end of the day.

"'Stupid idiot!' she'd yell, and she'd slap my face, if I dropped the glass milk bottle or coaxed our dog Pal to come clicking his toenails over the waxed linoleum floor or simply found ourselves in a wrong place, in her path, somehow, anywhere."

Uncle Don didn't remember their mother had been so harsh, and she'd always been kind to me. But in Depression-era family pictures, almost always, my grandma's mouth was stitched straight across her face, as if there were threads binding her lips and they wouldn't stretch wide enough to let her laugh or joke, not ever, and if there was an extreme to be had in that house, it was her, in a burst of fury that tore open the seam where her smile might have been. Dad's recollections could have been true.

In any case, I knew it was hard to care for him now. I thought back to a recent afternoon, when I was alerted to trouble by the sound of my father roaring from his bathroom: "NO!" he cried. "Panic! Panic!"

One of my own paid caregivers blocked the light with her bulk. With plastic-gloved hands, talking loud, she was trying to pull Dad to his feet from the toilet.

On Dad's other side was nurse Danny, purposeful and determined to be swift, after a long morning of trying to address Dad's impacted bowels, on and off and on and off the toilet. The twice-weekly suppository had been overlooked somehow, and five days of backed up waste had turned into immobile cement in his gut. Loud polka music issued from the CD player. There was too much going on in the room, a torrent of threatening sensation. I knew my father felt overpowered by the rush of caregiver instructions and his own physical discomfort.

He could not make the connection between the administration of a suppository and the relief that would come soon after. His experience was of brutal attack. So from the seat of the toilet, Dad fought for his very life, an old lion in a cage. He wanted to be safe and to feel some sense of autonomy. Since he could not, he roared.

I squatted before him, our faces level and our eyes locked, and tried to offer him a stream of translation and safety through my words.

"Dad, it's okay, you are safe, and I am right here to make sure of that, so please don't yell anymore. Let's get off the toilet, Danny is here to help us." Sometimes I could help him get through the fear and violation, talk him through the procedure, insist on his okayness, override his panic and his instinct to fight.

I could feel into the caregivers' experience too: exhausted, tense, too many patients, and now this old man holding onto the metal chair rail when he simply needed to let go. What might I say or do in their positions?

And I'd heard him yelling at them too.

"Dad, I heard you call our caregiver a ratty bitch."

He laughed in astonishment. "I can't believe it," he said.

"No," I agreed. "You rarely call people names."

He thought a minute. "But she was forcing me to do something I didn't want to do."

I wanted to keep these caregivers as allies and not project my judgment. The line wasn't always clear. Especially when my father was fighting with people who had responsibility for his physical care but had too many patients to tend and could not move as slowly as he required.

I needed to know who was hurting my father and to make it stop. Dad called her the "oink oink" person, because he said she called him a pig. Dad thought she was male, but I learned that she was a woman. I had met her before: she had very short hair and her voice was quite gruff, thus my father's gender confusion. We had talked about her life, and she'd told me she worked double shifts in the facility, 3:00 to 11:00 p.m., then 11:00 p.m. to 7:00 a.m., four or more days a week. In the eight hours she had off, she looked after her three-year-old grandson at home.

"I can't imagine how you keep going!" I said. "Your schedule isn't humanly possible!"

"I get by on four hours of sleep," she had told me. "But it's better than the night shift at Walmart, where I used to work before this." She was fifty-four years old, same as me. She earned $8.25 an hour, with no benefits and no paid time off for holidays or sick days. No wonder an old guy with his days and nights reversed sent her into a tailspin.

I was lucky to catch a slack tide on my weekly survey trip to the spoil island, which made for an easy paddle across the river's wide current. Only mid-May, but already so very hot. Sweat rolled down my neck and back, pasting my shirt to my skin. At either tip of the island, brown pelicans and terns loafed in good numbers, knee deep in the shallows.

Last week, I'd hit the tern jackpot. The high mound of soil in the center of the island was dotted with nesting least terns and a few gull-billed. I'd assembled my spotting scope quickly, so that I could make a rough count and leave them alone, for they were panicked and let me know of their displeasure by circling and calling and dive-bombing my head. At least thirty birds protected nests. As soon as I'd tallied them and clicked off a few pictures on my phone to document eggs, I'd squirmed off the spoil hill and walked back to my boat. I'd been thinking about them ever since, how they scrapped with one another over nesting space, delivered small fish to their mates, kept a group watch for predators.

Today I saved the center mound, the heart of the nesting tern territory, for last. When you survey nesting shorebirds, you watch for a spatial pattern. Least terns bound and rebound from the sand; that pattern is what cues you to locate the black heads of parents tending their eggs on the sand. The week before, I had counted thirty nesting pairs, along with several black skimmers and some gull-billed terns, and oystercatchers around the edge. All week long, I'd been replaying them in my mind.

Never did I imagine the terns would be gone. But it was true. The interior of the island where spoil had been piled highest was swept clean of terns. For a moment I wondered if I had really seen them the week before. But I had a picture of eggs on nests to prove it, and bird poop on my hat besides. And there had been many, many pairs. Adjusting my binoculars, I studied the ground, pausing to look closely at bits of plastic and other detritus shining on the sand. Could I have mistaken that garbage for terns on the ground? No way. The least terns had been everywhere, dive-bombing, chattering, and warning me away. West to east, horizon to horizon, I scoured the hill with my scope.

But there wasn't a single tern on the mound. What had happened? Not for the first time I chastised myself: I lived too far away to guard them. But never in a million years did I think they'd all be gone.

I raged across the river in my kayak, my heart beating wildly. Back in my truck, I dialed up Megan Lamb.

"Such a huge bummer, Megan. There wasn't a single least tern on the island just now," I said. "You know I saw thirty birds on the ground incubating last week, but today there are none at all."

I could hear her intake of breath. She was disappointed too.

"Why do you think?" I rushed along with my own train of thought. "Was Thursday's rain enough to flood the nests, even up high on the spoil? Could it have been predators? Raccoon? What do you think?"

"Oh, Sue, I'm afraid I can guess what happened," Megan replied. "My worst fear. Last weekend, someone organized an event called Paddlejam, right there in Apalachicola. The idea was to try and break the world record of the number of kayaks rafted together. It was billed as a fundraiser for at-risk youth by the local Methodist churches."

She continued. "I received several frantic phone calls on Saturday saying that the kayakers were told to stage on our spoil island before they made their kayak raft. By the time I got there, the kayak raft had already happened and no one was on island. I hoped the crowd hadn't been as bad as I imagined. Since the birds abandoned their nests, I'm afraid it was."

I dropped my forehead to the steering wheel of the truck, so hot it felt like a brand. It was a brand, the mark of the impotent, insufficient advocate.

I knew that those paddlers harbored no desire to disrupt the nesting shorebirds on the spoil island. But there are too many of us humans, and we don't (and don't know how to) calculate the needs of other species as we go about our lives.

I imagined the experience of those wild birds, nesting.

We all watch. At least one of us is always alert for the different thing, for the potential threat. The scared part of me that wants to live sees the man when he's only a dot crossing the water.

And when the boat tracks a straight line through the shoving waves and the sucking tide toward our beach, then my heart begins to pound, and my worry wakes the bird next to me, and the one next to her. The black skimmers are the first to scramble to their feet on the sand and fly. We terns unhook the single foot we have tucked and lifted into our bodies, and we pull our heads from beneath our wings. The pelicans open both eyes, not just one, and begin to shift their weight. And all of our hearts beat harder still.

Because the boat is coming straight at us and its colors frighten us—flaming orange and bright green. And because there is a flashing stick the human uses to propel himself straight toward our place on the open sand where we rest and mate and tend our eggs. There is no other place for us besides this length of sand. And so our hearts hammer in our chests. The skimmers unfurl their wings and test the air so they will be prepared when the final panic, the lift-urge overcomes them.

The man stands and unfolds his body from the boat. Nothing safe stands that tall on the sand, higher than the pelican's beak yawning and stretching to the sun, higher and stiffer than a great blue heron, higher and more threatening than we can bear. A few of us tolerate the fear longer than others. Others jump into the air and swoop and turn, "Aa— a-raw, aa-a-raw," we cry. And we will, all of us, leave our refuge, which no longer is one, because the man in the boat is pushing against our sand, the only place we can nest.

Surely he will understand from our voices and the displacement of our bodies that we are scared and that he must leave. But he does not. He lifts his pant leg and pees on our place and then he drags his boat farther onto the sand. Our sand. He studies the signs that have been placed to protect us, but he misunderstands, or else he wants what he wants, more than he understands. Legions of us lift. Our flightless chicks scurry for cover, and we cannot protect them, nor our eggs, now baking in the sun.

The man stretches his arms taller yet and surveys the beach. He pulls a tube of sunscreen from his pocket and sucks water from a bottle. Our voices are screaming and our blood is afraid and runs fast.

The man does not find what he was looking for, or he is bored, and so he drags his boat and his paddle through our place and slides his boat back into the sea—this time.

We are accustomed to the meander of the fins of dolphins in the water, and their leaping does not scare us, not even when they push mullet against the sand with their bodies. We accept the blood tax exacted by the eagle and the peregrine falcon. It is man and his dogs and the feral hogs he brought here that we may not survive.

Every time a human intrudes in this way into our small colonies, a cost is exacted from our nervous systems. Who will bring the human into right relationship with all the other beings? Who will?

How many, many times I have watched people walk right past protective barriers, right past the most beautiful interpretive signage we can create, straight into the tiny spaces we have managed to set aside for the wild birds to nest. Not everyone can be told what to do and then simply be left to their own devices. A commitment to kindness and respect has to come from some deeper cultural training; perhaps you have to be raised up in it. Somehow we must make this happen, because, as Kathleen Dean Moore has written, "This is the wonder-filled world that we are destroying, the lyric voices that we are silencing, the sanctity that we are defiling, at a rate and with a violence that cannot be measured."

Until people change their minds, deeply, deeply change, and understand and respect the equivalent needs of all species for life, all we can rely on is law enforcement. The enforcers—wildlife officers and volunteer stewards (and there are never enough of either)—are all we have to keep people out of the sacred nesting places. Without protection, ignorance and the desire to do whatever one pleases rule, and the bird or the old person suffers.

"My heart sinks when the least terns arrive in April and begin breeding—or trying to," a shorebird biologist told me recently. I understand his trepidation: the little birds' pugnacity is no match for beach-driving trucks, dogs, fireworks, and every manner of human intrusion into their nesting beaches. Shorebirds and seabirds are declining everywhere they exist, and some are already gone.

Like so many wild birds, least tern populations were decimated by hunters who shot them and sold their feathers to adorn women's hats. When the Migratory Bird Treaty Act was passed in 1918 and people began to change their attitudes toward conservation, least terns bounced back. But now, they are again so diminished by recreational, industrial, and residential development in their coastal breeding areas that they have been specially classified for protection in much of their North American range. No other wide-ranging North American tern has that unfortunate distinction.

Not every beach-going human dishonors the birds, and not every overworked caregiver is cruel. I was particularly grateful for the attentive watchfulness and advocacy of our helper Esmine. She was one of the gentlest people I knew, with an intuitive heart and a great capacity for patience. She was in her late forties, a strong woman with a lovely face. One afternoon, she and I stood beside Dad, and together helped him roll on his side so that Alisha, a wound-care specialist, could address a painful bedsore that had developed on Dad's left buttock.

We had been talking, Esmine and I, about how to ensure that my father was checked for dryness and turned regularly in his bed during the night. We despaired of it ever happening. We knew the facility's caregivers were paid minimum wage and overworked with no prospects of a raise. We knew many were rough and un-trained, as well. Their voices were not soft.

"I check on your dad when I'm here at night, to see that he's kept dry," Alisha said. "I keep these Landing girls on their toes," she said. I heard the "charge nurse" in Alisha's voice. I bet those workers jumped for her. Alisha was employed by a private company and was brought in as a consultant on hard-to-cure cases, like my dad's bedsores. Her hair, dyed golden, swept up from one ear and jaw to join a complex bun on the other side of her head. She looked like a queen.

In aspect, she was fierce, and in action, she was competent.

Alisha said: "I do an extra check on all my patients when I'm here at night. I think, what if these were my father or mother?" But these weren't Alisha's parents, they were very old, well-to-do, white people. I was surprised; I didn't know Alicia double-timed on night duty at the Landing. Dad yelped quietly as Alisha tended his wound.

"How can you work all day traveling between nursing homes doing wound care and then work twelve-hour night shifts?" I asked Alisha.

The two women exchanged a private glance: *you do what you have to do*. My friends and I compared notes about our sleep issues and our joint pains; too many of us had been treated for breast cancer, and most of us help with the care of our aging parents and grandchildren. But we took time off for vacations, and we had the resources we needed for health care. I so admired and loved Esmine and Alisha, who were as different from each other as any random pair of Caucasian women would be. I watched them carefully bandage Dad's sore, and I sensed a common steel to their spines and a loving kindness in their hearts that I leaned into and longed for. I felt humbled, like a child, and I knew I was a member of privileged class with an unearned, softer path.

I propelled my dad through the press of wheelchairs and walkers and costumed dogs and rolled him straight into his bathroom, facing the sturdy silver handgrip in the wall. He knew to grab the bar and pulled himself to his feet. I yanked the wheelchair out of the bathroom to give us working room. But Dad's brain would not allow him to execute the pivot to the toilet; he could not release his grip.

"Let go, Dad, let go," I cajoled, pressing my hip against his to offer a physical cue. If he felt the porcelain commode at the back of his knees, I thought, he would feel safe enough to negotiate a forty-five-degree turn and sit. Instead, he did a deep knee bend in place, as if honoring the wall, still clutching the bar. Sweat prickled the back of my neck.

"Dad, you need to turn," I said.

"I am, Sue, I am!" The connection between his will and his nerve endings was blocked or broken. I couldn't reach the red button that would enable me to summon help without letting go of Dad. This maneuver was all on us.

I pushed my hair away from my face, clamped the back of Dad's shirt in case he fell, and scanned the room for any kind of solution. I spotted the hospice-provided chair potty behind the shower curtain. "Hey, Dad, here's an idea," I said to my frozen-in-place father. With my free right hand, I dragged the portable stool from the stall.

"I can't hold out much longer," Dad growled. I juggled the potty over my head and beneath his trembling thighs.

"Sit down, Dad, just let yourself relax," I urged. He was going to miss the bowl but cleaning up pee didn't worry me. Finally, he sat.

The Puppy Parade was still on my mind, whether as entertainment for Dad or social obligation, I cannot tell you why. So I hurried him. Peeled off his shoes, socks, sweatpants, and diaper. Worked soothing cream into his pressure sore. Slid clean pull up over his ankles, followed by fresh socks, soft sweatpants, and dry Hush Puppies. I persuaded him to stand at the bar again, so that I could push a towel around the floor with the toe of my shoe, to absorb the sheet of urine that hadn't made it into the pot.

Helping Dad at this stage of his disease was like dressing the Patty Playpal dolls my sister and I had begged for and received from our parents when we were nine and ten years old. The dolls were tall, the size of large toddlers, molded from hard plastic. Mine had shoulder-length brown acrylic hair. Like Dad, her joints didn't flex.

CHAPTER 15

Puppy Parade

When we were children, our mother had taught us to hug and
cession of family pets, in particular a pair of long-lived, poo
shepherds. Dad remembered those untrained animals for the
in our neighborhood. So I was surprised when the Landing s
ther's New Year's resolution: to pat more dogs. They hoped l
event they called "Puppy Parade."

When I came to fetch him for the festivities, my father's he
neck like a flower too heavy for its stalk. A strand of spittle
cord to his chest. He slept like a stone in his chair. The kinc
would have been to let him rest, but I felt obliged to rouse
Parade.

Within the circle of twenty-five residents and guests sat f
dents, women I'd never seen before in the facility. At least fi
died during the last six months.

"Dad, look!" I pointed out the parade contenders lining u
dozen miniature dogs with nametags pinned to their costu
Milo and Barnaby), leashed and low to the ground. "Love T
yipping of the gathered pack. Tank, an extra-thick dachshun
ouflage cape, sniffed the nether regions of Sweetness, some ki
outfitted as a garnet-and-gold-clad cheerleader. This could be
in a dreary winter week.

Dad turned to me. "Sue, I have to go to the bathroom. N
urgent. I felt my impatience rise. He was the guest of hono
he received suppositories every three days to loosen his col
request seriously.

Dad has one up on Patty Playpal, I thought to myself. *At least his knees can bend. Sometimes.*

I coached my father back into the wheelchair.

"Do you want to catch the end of the Puppy Parade?"

"Sure." He was always a sport.

Back to the living room we rolled. The show was over, except for the final scoring. Biscuits had been dispensed to each resident to reward the dogs, whether they had "won" or not. I watched Miss Annie take a bite out of one of the treats she held. Dad didn't try to eat his doggy stick but neither did he reach down and feed it to one of the contenders. Nor did he pet a dog.

Ashley asked if we'd like her to run through the script again, just for us.

"No thanks," Dad said.

Back in the room, I set up cheese and crackers and some cider on my father's tray, but he was too exhausted to eat.

I hailed the young, kind Hispanic caregiver passing in the hall. "Hey Jackie, can you give us a hand?"

"We don't need help," said Dad. "I just want to dive into my bed." That was an old trick that had trapped him on his hands and knees in the past. I insisted. At my signal, Jackie lifted his legs onto the bed.

"Now we are going to turn you over," I said. We logrolled him onto his side. Then I perched next to my father on the bed, both of us worn, and to what end? Even I felt stiff and frustrated, but I was able-bodied and could freely choose anything I desired that moment: to move in and out of the patch of sun shining in on Dad's comforter; to reach for a handful of almonds on the bedside table; and later, to slice and stir vegetables for my dinner with Jeff.

"I could just weep," my father said, and I noticed his cheek was wet. I wiped it dry with a tissue. "I don't see how my head can process all my tears," he said.

I had wronged him with all that forcing. I stroked his head, realizing that while it was hard to be in the position of caregiver, it was nowhere near as challenging as being conscious inside a body whose brain is unable to direct its own movements. My job wasn't to simply manipulate my father's limbs, his clothes, his caloric intake, his caregiver schedule. Entertainment shouldn't be my highest priority.

I understood the pattern better when I watched other people overdo. On a Wednesday morning, I dropped by the Landing to deliver supplies to Dad's room.

My father was balanced on the very edge of his bed, his eyes tightly squeezed shut. He was flanked by two caregivers, who looked as if they were holding up a 140-pound sack of flour between them. He had that little muscle tone. He was far, far away inside his head and would not respond to my greeting.

The two women were flushed and damp with effort, both wearing disposable neoprene gloves. One was trying to wrestle a blue denim shirt over his T-shirt. My father's elbow was bent like a chicken's wing, and it seemed to me that unless he either relaxed or woke up and participated, that shirt would never go on his body.

"Why not try a stretchy cardigan sweater," I suggested, and so they did. Then he was hoisted into his wheelchair, and from there to his recliner.

That was another thing: when I wasn't in the room as much, the caregivers squabbled, some of them. About trading shifts, about who should take out the trash, or shave my father—or not. About who stayed too long after her shift ends, just to boss and annoy the next. About whose blood pressure had shot to 170/129 from the stress of it all. Was it my job to care for them too? In this room, with this impossible task, we were all laid bare—our essential selves—by the slow duty of caring for this man as he inevitably declined. Each woman tried, I knew, to match my expectation to give Dad as much dignity and quality of life as possible. Each one of them shone like the purely minted love they were, each in their own way, some of the time.

And me, I kept wrestling with: how do I know what is enough? Dad's illness was a puzzle I believed I must solve.

I said to my friend Norine: "It's just that I know that I have the power to make Dad's life so much better!"

She replied: "But this is your father's life, Susan. There is no way you can make it all right for him. Your dad will have to negotiate this bleak landscape, what looks like a moonscape, himself."

Another friend told me how her demented father had become needy and frightened, even though he still lived independently in an apartment. He had begged her to take over his care. She traveled periodically to see him, but she told him bluntly: "Dad, I am not your caregiver, or your mother or your wife. I want to remain in relationship with you as your adult child."

The following week, I requested—and was granted—hospice care for my dad. At that time, the hospice industry was growing steadily and I knew many people who

A healthy red knot in fine breeding condition. Photo by David Moynahan.

had benefited from its services. We didn't believe he was close to death, but he'd lost significant weight and muscle mass, and the extra attention would help. A hospice music therapist serenaded him, and a home health aide helped with bathing. And others: clergy, nurse, social worker, each one so very kind.

Dad was deeply startled: "I thought hospice was for people who are dying?" he said. The caregivers were uneasy too. Beulah said she felt like the buzzards were circling. Jill noticed that when hospice personnel were in the room, the Landing staff vanished, leaving him in wet clothes in bed. Had I made a mistake? Had I misjudged how the balance of what we had in place might be thrown off by bringing on more help, especially people attuned to the dying process?

The next Saturday, buoyed by Dad's extra resources, and therefore, our freedom, Jeff and I launched our boat in Apalachicola to walk a remote outer stretch of St. Vincent Island.

A red knot hunkered down at the water's edge, a bundle of feather and bone pressed against the sand. We'd been admiring the knots as they moved through north Florida on their migration, five to ten at a time, mostly. They fed voraciously, plunging their bills over and over into the wet sand at the water's edge, reminding me of a host of paper doll birds, so alike was one to the next. But this one had been stopped short in her unimaginably long travels (at least six nonstop days and nights of flight) from the high Arctic to the tip of South America. She had been unable to find and gorge on horseshoe crab eggs and other foods that would allow her to recover and regain weight. This bird wasn't going to make it.

Her eyes slitted shut, and her bill opened and closed rhythmically. I crouched at a distance that wouldn't add to her distress, watching her sip the last breaths of air she would ever inhale. Now and again she trembled.

But she was not dying alone.

A sanderling, feisty loner of the winter beach, had nestled in the sand near the knot's head. I'd never seen a sanderling assume such a position, though surely they do when they incubate their own eggs. Then a second red knot took up a post at the rear flank of the downed bird. Two lesser yellowlegs (tall shorebirds uncommon on this beach) moved in, intervening between the small sheeting waves of the Gulf and the knot. They tilted their heads sideways, ascertaining the knot's situation, and then simply stood close.

The four vigil birds—only one a conspecific—were companioning the rare red knot as she died. My human mind ran through its paces. First, as a citizen scientist, I thought I should look for identifying color flags or bands, because red knots are so highly endangered. But her feet were tucked under her body, and I was not going to pick up this bird during her dying. That would be extraordinarily stressful and disrespectful, as well. Then I wondered for just a moment if we should try to take the bird to a wildlife rehabilitator. Considering the eight bumpy miles we had to travel by back to the ramp and then who knows how far by car to find help—that trauma was out of the question, as well. My impulse to rescue was contradicted by the impossibility of capturing and stressing the bird in its final hours.

After a few minutes, I didn't stare at the bird anymore. I relieved it of my fierce attention and replaced that with love and compassion. The four vigil birds showed me what to do: simply be with. Simply offer tender presence to the incapacitated one. They taught me how to bear witness, and their bodies blurred through my tears. As I sat quietly on the sand, I watched the sun glimmer on the yolky limbs of the yellowlegs. The wind lifted the delicately barred back feathers of the downed and dying knot. The tide continued its rise. We all continued to breathe. Silently,

I renewed my vow to work on the behalf of all the shorebirds still tying our planet together with their journeys.

In the same way, even with hospice in place, decisions regarding Dad's care and treatment weren't always clear. Death by dementia, we were learning, was a very slow process, even if you'd finally accepted its inevitability.

On a cold afternoon in February, the Landing called: "Your dad has fallen, significant face wound, you may want to come in." I traded out my exercise clothes for warm hospital layers and entered a chaotic scene in Dad's room. The space was crowded. Luke, the handyman, was there with his rug shampooer and a bottle of OxiClean; several Landing caregivers and the bus driver stood by. Our caregiver had turned her back on Dad briefly, just as a stray impulse propelled him out of his wheelchair onto the floor, by way of a sharp-cornered hospital table.

Blood was pooling into Dad's left eye, but he squinted at me through the right, very happy I'd arrived. "Could we take care of this with butterfly bandages and avoid another hospital ordeal?" I wondered out loud.

"No," said Danny the nurse. He wiped away the blood and showed me two impressive gashes. Band-Aids wouldn't suffice.

An ambulance was summoned. I called a retired doctor friend to help me practice saying no to unnecessary tests or procedures in the emergency room. Just as I'd feared, the emergency room doctor wanted to prescribe a CT scan to check for bleeding under the skull, a subdural hematoma. What would they do if there was one, I asked? "We'd perform surgery to drain out the blood," the doctor said. "Which would require a brief hospital stay for your father."

I edged my body so I could block Dad from a necessary conversation I needed to have with the doctor. "My father has been on and off hospice three times, and we have a do-not-resuscitate order," I said. "I do not want to seem irresponsible or cause his death, but my dad has just turned eighty-eight, and he doesn't do well with anesthesia or overnight stays in hospitals. We'll take just the stitches, please." A woman known as the "sew 'em up" nurse agreed to add Dad to her queue before her dinner break.

Dad's gashes zigged across his forehead, zagged down the bridge of his nose. But he didn't flinch when the nurse stuck a needle of Novocain right into the pink flesh parting his brow—it was at least three quarters of an inch deep. "That was painless," he said.

The nurse was a tender wizard. She showed me how she decided where to place each suture. "You can't sew a continuous straight line as if you were hemming a dress, because then if it fails in one place you lose the whole line," she explained.

When she had packed up her gear and left, our spate of good luck came to a halt. It took another hour and a half to nudge someone to apply a line of antibiotic to Dad's stitches, do the paperwork to release us, and help us figure out how to return Dad to his facility. We hadn't taken him outside the facility in more than a year because he had so little body tone. Jeff and I simply couldn't manage his physical transfer into one of our cars. I learned that although ambulances will bring you to the hospital, they will not take you back home.

"Your nursing home is required to figure this out for you," said the unhelpful girl in the nurses' station. I called the Landing and left a message on the answering machine. "We are helping other patients, please leave a message," the recording said.

Jeff brought us take-out dinner, but as the hours passed, Dad became more and more restless and was losing coherence. I called the nursing home director twice at her home. Over the phone, I could hear her baby screaming—it was her bedtime too. "This time of night," said Ashley, "we have no one on staff who can bring Bob back home. I'm so sorry."

Like flies on tarpaper, we were trapped.

The unhelpful girl at the nurses' station said: "If you have $150 in cash, one of those freelance stretcher transport companies will *probably* take him home." Finally, Jeff cajoled a male nurse to help him lift Dad into my car. When I pulled out of the brightly lit parking garage, Dad said, "It looks like the Newark airport terminal!" He hadn't been out in the nighttime streets in several years. It was 10:00 p.m. before we managed one final heroic lift to get Dad out of the car and into his wheelchair, finally, his own bed.

Back in our own home, I watched my husband pack his duffel for a three-day sampling trip in North Carolina. Jeff was near tears, telling me about the new Florida governor's proposal to cut growth management in Florida. We had planned a cozy fireside night together over a leftover chili supper and Netflix. At least we had those options and dreams.

The outcome of my father's life was clear, but not the timing of the end. Despite the stitches Dad had just endured, we had begun to see that death by dementia was not a death by a thousand cuts but, as David Shenk writes in *The*

Forgetting, "by a thousand subtractions." Here is another way the catastrophe of human dementia parallels the incomprehensible losses we are perpetrating on the biosphere that is our only home. In both cases, a universe is smothered: living fibers and cells in the human brain, and millions of species on the Earth—of which the red knot and the American oystercatcher and the snowy plover are only a few. As we plow the rainforests and heat the oceans and the air, we destroy (subtract) incalculably complicated webs of interdependent connections. We unravel the world at our certain peril.

CHAPTER 16

Pear Mudra

When you pushed through the Landing's enormous double doors on a lonely Sunday, a gauntlet of residents lined the foyer to greet you. This day, a great wedge of man with one eye patched, the other squinting (a pirate come to the nursing home), stood watch. He fixed his good eye on the square bakery box I carried. "Cookies?" he guessed. "Cake?" It was my birthday, and I'd brought treats for Esmine and Dad.

In a nearby chair sat Miss Annie. A white pop-bead necklace circled her throat. I squeezed her hand and she took my mine and turned it between her own two palms. "My land!" she said, and then she studied my hand some more and then she said, "My gracious! My goodness gracious!" The words caught a little on her dentures. Miss Annie was always ready for delight, this time the simple fact of my warm hand in hers. Not so much that I paused to greet her but that this thing—my hand—had passed suddenly into her world. But I had to keep walking toward my own father, down the long halls and around two corners. "Goodbye, Miss Annie, I'll see you soon," I said, withdrawing my hand.

"Sue!" My father cried. "You came home!" From his recliner, Dad, dressed in a sleeveless wool vest over a flannel shirt, opened his arms, inviting me to come close and hug him. I'd noticed how he physically reached for what he wanted now, stretched his arms out slowly, first his right, then his left to meet the desired object, whether a navel orange or a daughter.

I inhaled the familiar aroma of his neck. A friend had asked me: "Don't you miss your father the way he was before his illness, the person you knew as your father?"

Dad's last birthday, 2011. Photo by Jeff Chanton.

But no: his physical diminishment had not altered his essence, nor the big love in his heart.

"Your dad, he was just telling me how sad he is," Esmine said.

"Why are you sad, Dad?" I backed away from his embrace so that I could look into his eyes.

"He says he is homesick," Esmine replied. "He was wishing his children were here. I told him I was sure you would come today." And there I was, with pastries, to celebrate my birthday with my father.

"Pick which dessert you'd like," I said.

Dad pointed to the red velvet chocolate cupcake with sugar butter icing and tiny red sprinkles. Esmine selected a square of carrot cake.

"We were singing before you came in." She passed us each a napkin.

"Ahhhh . . . Ohhhhh . . . Ahhhh . . ." Dad broke into a kind of chant, just as natural and unnatural as could be.

"Before that one, we were singing the amen song," Esmine said.

Dad fell into his cupcake, a total sensory experience. I knew he couldn't eat something that delicious and focus on conversation at the same time, so I unpacked groceries (four boxes of Kleenex, cheese crackers, and dish soap) and checked his bowel movement chart (X-large, loose, 1/28). Even on a holiday or birthday, my visits were always a combination of scanning his supplies, health, the caregiver log, and being as present as possible with Dad, the man himself.

I reached for Dad's empty plate, and then Esmine's.

"Many nights as I gather and stack the supper plates to return to the kitchen, your father will ask me where I'm going," Esmine told me. "He'll say, 'Don't bother, I'll take care of the clean up tonight.'" Dad's lifelong habit was to be of service. Now he could do almost nothing for himself. But he still owned the impulse to help.

One Sunday I sat with him alone. Often the words didn't come easily for him, and I would search for small things that might engage us both. No longer did I expect to learn new family secrets or insights. Still, it was the fall equinox, the day my mother had died in 1975, so I blurted out what came to my mind. "Dad," I said, "It's been thirty-four years today since Mom died." The end of her life was a mystery I still wished I could solve.

"That was a really awful time for you, wasn't it, Dad?"

"You know it," he said. And no more.

Even with hospice support, it had taken several years to relieve Dad of the pharmaceuticals that had extended his life without improving its quality. Goodbye to Namenda, Aricept, Metformin. Farewell Finasteride and aspirin. No more cups of crushed bitter pills hidden in ice cream or applesauce or pudding. All banished from his chart, except Seroquel to sleep and suppositories to poop, thus honoring my father's own wishes.

In response, ministrokes stepped up their lightning in his brain. I witnessed one myself. Dad stopped suddenly in his walker and said, "Sue, I can't move." Then he began to shudder, as if in a seizure. It passed, and he was able to resume stepping back to his room. Other times, strokes would leave him listing far to the left or the right in his chair. Almost always, there'd be a general weakening of muscle tone, and one time, he lost his language. That, for me, was a tragedy.

All the visual cues were still there—the facial movements that accompany spoken word, spoken thought, thought made audible and then received. He'd try to vocalize and his eyes would widen just slightly at the right place in his "speech" to express . . . what? His brows would lift, and his smile would widen, and he might reach for my hand, but all language had vanished.

I realized how so often I'd been able to complete a fragment of a sentence he'd begun: "I need to use" or simply "I need" or "I've been thinking." Like a writing prompt I'd use to stimulate my own language, maybe I'd see him twitch at his gray sweatpants and I'd guess. "Want something to eat, Dad?" Yes, or no, he'd say.

What should be my proper response now, when every word and phrase was garbled and I simply couldn't understand? Should I pretend I did? That seemed wrong, but I couldn't keep saying, "I don't know what you mean, Dad." Or "What did you say, Dad?" And if he couldn't verbalize a train of thought, did that mean he wasn't having one? Did that mean he wasn't understanding my words either?

Previously, when Dad's physical body was immobilized with ministrokes, we'd still been able to admire his expressive vocabulary and his humor. All that was stripped away. When the words were all gone and only a scramble of sound accompanied the language of his long-loved face, that felt unbearable to me. My friend Crystal said: "Of course you are grieving that loss. Language, words, that's what you had left with him." And language, words—they were my work.

A week or so later, on an evening visit, I asked if he was hungry, not expecting a reply.

"We had a voluminous dinner tonight," he said.

I laughed out loud. "Dad's back," I grinned at Esmine. "At least for now."

Still, the room felt excruciatingly small. Only the caregivers moved and spoke at any length, and the windows remained closed. But those five women covered all of Dad's waking hours, from seven in the morning until nine at night. They tended him far more than I did now.

I visited him not as a caregiver but as a daughter. It was hard, especially when Esmine would report: "What he wants is to be with his family." But what Dad and I could do together and what I could do there now felt too confining. I was so grateful for our staff of helpers. But I didn't want their jobs.

Jeff and I drove south to the Florida Snow Ball, as we did each winter, to Gulfport. There, the Casino Ballroom perches on the north shore of Boca Ciega Bay, a water body so urbanized that its tiny swath of sand is highly prized and precious, to both people and shorebirds.

A really good contradance is the closest I've come to flying in a flock of shorebirds. In this kind of dance, you and your partner move with another couple through a series of figures with evocative names like Mad Robin, Box the Gnat, California Twirl, Ocean Wave, and Hey for Four.

What transforms a contra from a series of rote steps to a transcendent experience is the ability of the group to synchronize. You need a room full of people working together and moving in time to music. When a great caller and a fabulous live band drive the steps into your body memory, that synchrony can happen. It feels to me like being in a company of wild birds.

From where we whirled on the white maple ballroom floor, I could see assemblages of black skimmers, willets, and several varieties of gull resting on the beach. They were as connected to one another as the dancers inside.

But unlike the dancers and the Gulfport beachgoers, the birds' options were severely limited. We humans could twirl in the ballroom or walk along the shore for pleasure, even get in the car and drive away, but those shorebirds required the beach for sleeping, feather care, eating, and nesting. The restive and rare birds—like the black skimmers—were the first to be displaced. Willets and sanderlings will sometimes skip ahead and then double back to the same feeding spot after danger passes, but the shyest species will not. Where else can the birds rest and feed? Human disturbance was—is—rendering the beach almost unusable to its original inhabitants.

Each time I caught a glimpse of the birds swirling into the air and describe currents in space with their bodies, I knew that something had scared them off the sand. In this urban setting, the birds weren't moving for the pleasure of flocking in flight: inevitably it was because humans and their dogs walked oblivious, right through the shorebirds' assemblies. Sometimes I saw people even run and stamp at the rare congregations of birds, just to see them fly, or to take pictures, reducing the living beings to mere spectacle, and I'd want to run outside and scream at them.

At Snow Ball, we learned a new dance figure: Yearn Left. We stood in a line of couples, holding hands, facing a long row of other pairs. The caller directed us to feel pulled . . . drawn . . . to the couple standing on the left diagonal.

"Let the emotion of yearning draw you forward to that next couple you will be dancing with," he explained. "The Yearn is a very simple movement but full of longing." As we incorporated the figure into a sequence with others we already knew, the caller gradually withdrew his words. Through the microphone came just a whispered hint to remind us of our next move.

"*Sssss . . .*" he whispered, when it was time to Circle Right. "*Hhhhhh-aaay . . .*" for Hey for Four, and then "*Y-y-y-ya . . .*" and we knew it was time to Yearn. As for the shorebirds, a group mind gradually infused the dance and the dancers with elastic, joyful connection.

I believe the yearning so many of us feel has to do with all the ways we've been cut off from the natural world. We yearn for the Eden that Earth was, for who we were as a species and all that surrounded us. But our yearning has distorted that original understanding, and we take and we take.

A first step to healing our loneliness is to pay attention to and honor the needs of all of Earth's life-forms. There they are: right outside the window!

The requirements of Dad's care became increasingly subtle, and those caregivers not given to deep patience, or a sense of humor, and the ability to go slowly, weren't doing so well on their shifts. His intentions and desires were intensely felt but often inscrutable.

Just as I was learning to anticipate the needs of wild birds, I saw how Esmine would respond to cues and clues that were tiny but true. She'd say: "Okay, Mr. Isleib, it's time to get into bed, but I'll need you to help me." He might say, "I'm just too weak tonight," but still he'd move at her direction. Esmine never forced Dad and neither did Jill.

Jill told me that she was glad when her schedule allowed a day spent with him from waking until bedtime. It helped her understand his rhythms, impulses, and moods, she said. She found that in his grumpy times, she could help him into his wheelchair, and he'd scoot around the room propelled by his feet, always backward; every now and then he'd pull himself forward by gripping the edge of a table, hand over hand. In these ways, he could move about without being lifted or hauled like a sack of grain from one chair to another or to the bed. Jill would play some polka music on the CD player and open a book, and from time to time they would catch each other's eyes and smile. I still imagine their faces in my mind.

I'd been with him very little in the weeks since the release of my new book. I stopped in one evening and found him lying flat in his recliner chair. Esmine sat beside him. We raised the back of his chair and talked. Dad hugged me close against his chest.

Esmine left the room to let us visit. Dad reached for my hands and twined them in his, crossing our wrists. His palms were smooth and warm. Then he began to pull himself up to seated, using the strength of my hands. He'd rise a full six inches, as if doing an abdominal core exercise, and then release back down to his recliner. His movements were snakelike: rhythmic, continuous, unfolding, his hands moving across mine. Sitting up, relaxing back. Crossing and uncrossing his left knee over his right.

Suddenly, he opened his eyes and stared into mine, fully present, his blue eyes bluer next to his checked flannel shirt.

"Is it almost over?" he asked.

"What do you think, Dad?" We talked about how tired he was of that disease.

"But what will happen next?" he asked. And then: "I really miss my mother and father."

"You haven't seen them in such long time, have you?" I said.

We sat close for the better part of an hour, his hands winding over mine like moving vines.

"How do my hands look to you?" I asked.

"Gnarly!" he said, and we laughed. This dying wasn't always so serious.

In the New Leaf Market, young produce workers rotated out week-old pears, which often appeared whole and perfect to my eye. These they replaced with fruit from a just-opened box of the same variety. The box bore a label from Oregon. Each salmon red pear was nestled separately in soft tissue, like breakable eggs might be. I asked if I could choose one from those just arrived, to purchase. The young men, deep in conversation, smiled and waved permission.

In my father's room, I sliced one perfect pear into lengthwise quarters on the gray metal hospital table. The pear had a firm, mealy consistency, a heft to its pure fruit sugar. It glistened with the Oregon rainwater its mother tree had pulled from the ground, maybe somewhere on the shoulders of Mount Hood. I scooped out the seeds and the root of the slim black stem and handed a section to my dad. That fresh fruit, so different from the processed industrial food provided by the facility, lit up the taste buds in his mouth. He consumed all four quarters. I cut open a second pear.

When the fruit was gone, my dad's fingertips continued to ferry emptiness to his lips. Nothing except the memory of the freshest of pears entered his mouth. That gesture of sacred self-feeding, and the mudra of emptiness enclosed by his thumb and middle forefinger—they touched me.

CHAPTER 17

Thin Places

"What do you see?" I asked my father on short, dim winter's solstice eve.

"A bright light glowing," he said. I could discern no source of illumination save the lamp between us.

His dreams and visions were what we had left between us. They grew ever more fragmentary in the reporting but sufficed to let me know where his unconscious was taking him.

"I dreamed . . ." said Dad. His voice strengthened. "I dreamed I was walking down Hamilton Avenue." That was the street in Glen Rock, New Jersey, where my father had lived with his family as a boy.

"How old were you in the dream?" I asked.

"Seventeen," he said.

"Who else was there?"

"My mother and Billy Joe Francis," he said. Many times during Dad's last months, he asked me if I remembered Billy Francis. I came to think of Billy as one of Dad's angels, though I knew only the barest facts about him from Dad and Uncle Don.

Dad said that Billy was known as Hot Dog Francis because his father ran a local delicatessen. Billy was an only child; he enlisted in the army during World War II at age twenty. Not long after, he died in a Miami hospital, not on a European battlefield, of malaria. He came home in a box just as dead as if a bullet had killed him. Dad wrote a four-page letter of condolence to Billy's heartbroken parents. Now Billy Joe Francis was at Dad's side, keeping my father company deep in the wakeful night.

My father's room had grown dense with his stasis, with his enforced stillness in chair or bed. His lungs and throat sometimes filled with phlegm, which he would clear by coughing. The pothos plant in the corner had ranged and curled to fill the space between the window and his bed. It presided over a filing cabinet whose only function now was to hold up the plant, his radio, and sometimes, at night, his glasses. I would bring fruit to occupy myself when I visited, slicing apples, a navel orange, a pint of strawberries into a glass bowl.

"Who's here in the room with us?" he asked. He'd been reporting visits from his father and mother to our caregivers.

"No one, Dad, it's just you and me."

But that wasn't his experience. His eyes startled open wide.

"Huh?" He leaned forward in his chair, uncrossed his knees, and stared into the empty corner of the room. His bare shins protruded from the soft gray of his sweatpants.

"Oh, okay," he said, confidently, nodding his head. "Yes."

He turned back to me with a report.

"That was your grandma," he said. "Didn't you see her standing at the door? She was waving at me, but I wasn't completely sure what I was supposed to do. Do you think she was telling me to stay or to come with her?"

Candace McKibben, a dear friend and hospice minister, had told me what Dad was experiencing weren't hallucinations but "thin places," life moments when a person senses a connection with something far beyond the ordinary realms.

"The dying are most often visited by their mothers," she confirmed. How much sense it made that the woman whose body was our gateway into the physical world might be once again present as we take our final breaths.

Near the end of the nesting season, I experienced another kind of a thin place, on the spoil island. I had made my way around the tiny landscape with my spotting scope over my shoulder and binoculars around my neck, moving slowly, keeping count of all the birds I saw. On earlier visits, I'd seen pairs of oystercatchers slipping around like shadows, so I looked for them in particular. Just as soon as my eyes keyed in on the shape of a large ebony bird sitting on the sand, it startled away. How fearsome I was to that parent bird, with my spiderlike tripod and upright slow-moving body. Imagine if the only way we could protect our newly born was to draw the predator away with our own bodies and our own voices, implying, *There's no nest, no chicks, no eggs, keep your eye on me, let me draw you far away from what I am trying to bring into the world.*

I fixed in my mind where I first spotted the bird and advanced carefully over the sand to a place triangulated between a broken bit of plastic bucket and a certain white morning glory blossom.

And there they were: two eggs marbled brown and black, as fragile and unlikely as snowflakes on the sand. An extra high tide could so easily wash them away. A crow or a large gull could devour them. Or if all went well, this line of oystercatchers might continue another generation.

Away I went, on around the island. Eventually, I found three nests, and in the last of them, I witnessed life crossing between the worlds.

It was the tip of the bill of an oystercatcher chick meeting the salt air for the very first time. At first, I thought the hole meant that the egg must be damaged. Had ants punctured it, or was the eggshell thinned and then fractured by the weight of the parents' bodies? But no: there at the center of the hole, a tiny bill, a new rare life, was entering our world.

I allowed myself only the barest moment to ascertain what I saw, for the adults were circling wide, silent arcs out over the water and back. I needed to leave the eggs under the protection of their own parents, even though my instinct was to kneel down and stay. Kneel down and pray. Though I wasn't welcome to watch, I knew the full hatch of that chick, its first tumble onto the sand, would be as miraculous and sacred as the birth of any other species on Earth. I paddled away from the island, awash in gratitude and awe.

In the end, my father's death was a similar crossing. A final virus commandeered Dad's lungs, and with it the illness that would end his life. Those last few days, although his body labored, my dad didn't appear to be in pain. A nurse gave me possession of the liquid morphine to administer as I felt it was needed. We sang to him, stroked his face and his hands. As he took one last breath, his lids flew open, and one last glance of his gray eyes swept our faces. I saw his body ensouled, and then I saw his corpse, spirit gone. Like an eggshell, his physical frame was left behind for us to oil, and wrap in cloth, and bury in the ground. His soul, like

Priceless: the nest and eggs of an American oystercatcher. Photo by the author.

the dark chick, had fled. I stepped from the room to call David. His grandpa, my father, was dead.

Some days later, on a quiet stretch of Gulf beach, I curled on the sand as if a bird in an egg. I laid my head on my notebook and covered my binoculars with my shirt. There were no sounds except the crumble of small waves on the strand. Their comings and goings, their rhythmic whooshing called to mind a womb, interior waters, first home. It was the shush of oneness before birth, and perhaps after death as well. In between, and for now, I'd found my own thin place.

CHAPTER 18

Saving the World

"How would you like me to inscribe your book?" I asked the woman across the long folding table. "Is it a gift for someone else, or for you personally?" I had just delivered a talk about advocacy, and now it was time to sell and sign books.

"Just tell me what to do to save Florida," she said. "Just write that down for me."

I have been plotting and working and writing my way toward that question my whole adult life. And yet, Florida, and my state's wildlife, the Earth herself—all the things I dearly loved and wished I could protect—seem no closer to being "saved" than they were before I began. Perhaps *saving* is the wrong verb.

A man—white, heavyset, dressed in a pumpkin-orange shirt—raised his hand from the back of an auditorium in Clearwater, Florida. There was a logo stitched on his breast pocket, but he stood so far back in the darkened rows of chairs, I couldn't read the words, or the expression on his face. I wondered if he was a heckler or a fan. My talk had been wide ranging: Standing Rock, climate change, the Trump administration's attacks on the environment, and need for urgent, radical change.

His question: What is the single most important thing that every one of us should do right now, given all that confronts us?

I pulled down deep inside myself for an answer.

What I said: Don't turn away. Face what threatens the unborn of all species with all of your strength and all of your heart.

Sometimes, that can be a beautiful thing. The first week of August offered me and Jeff an unexpected respite from summer's heat. It was windy and cool at the coast, so we took our boat to the far end of the refuge and rafted in the shade of Cabbage Top for the longest time. This small floating cathedral had been the first place I had truly come to terms with the irrevocable rise of the sea. But still, we returned to it, and always it was lovely. This particular day, the palms talked and talked in the wind. Hordes of small dragonflies used the protection of the palm fronds, as we did, to stay in place. On every horizon, cumulus storms columned to the sky.

Our task is to watch over the world with such care.

One fall day, Jeff and I searched out the last snowy plover chick hatched on the refuge that season. In her small roving body rested the last chance that year for our landscape to contribute to a continuity of plovers, a single bird begun as an egg laid on this very sand.

I'd seen that chick and her parent on an earlier survey one week before, near the outfall of Oyster Creek. Just now, though, the beach seemed empty of everything but trash, and more trash. We picked up two enormous loads of plastic bottles and balloons in the green net fish bags we keep for that purpose. We saw no chick. I assumed she had been snatched by gull or ghost crab, vanished like all the others this season into the belly of a predator.

We circled back toward the east, toward Little St. George Island, to continue our search. And there she was, flashing across the strand, her tiny body skittering and zooming as she snapped at small flies. We followed her path with our binoculars, and she led us to a glorious surprise: 150 black terns, paused on their southbound journey to winter on the coast of South America. To my eye, they resembled small ebony sails temporarily furled. Sleek and gray and unexpected on the white of our sand. I'd never seen so many before.

It was a good place for that plover chick, threading through those black terns and a handful of others—least, Caspian, royal, gull-billed—all paused on the outer edge, between their summer and winter lands. I saw many fewer ghost crabs on the evanescent edge; the absence of their swift claws would give the chick a better shot at survival. Still: the last of the chicks, the last of the black terns.

In the 1920s, Arthur Bent described the black tern as the "most widely distributed, most universally common, and most characteristic summer resident of the sloughs, marshes and wet meadows of the [Dakota] plains." Since the 1960s, black

My husband, Jeff, with our boat at Cabbage Top, St. Vincent National Wildlife Refuge.
Photo by the author.

terns have been declining at the rate of 2 or 3 percent each year. I have seen them only here and on the leading edge of Little Saint George, their wings beating while the tips of their toes still touched the refuge, which was disappearing as well.

And yet, would I turn away from them? Never. We must linger longer, watching the beautiful things, watch them with exquisite attention, praying that their spirits will inform our actions on their behalf and our own.

As the sun began to angle into the sea, I thought about how our planet and our sun had created such palettes on uncounted nightfalls, long before these plovers or I had come to be. Earth has turned in far lonelier eons, without bird or human. I staggered under a gratitude so weighty that I had to sink to my heels, for I had the privilege to share this time with the creatures I loved.

The flaming sun lit up the whole of my face. The wind lifted my hair. I closed my eyes and became simply another breathing presence on the sand. No boundaries.

In our saltwater and bones bodies, each one of us loves the birds this much. They have companioned us through the Holocene, weavers of current and nest cup. Their songs were our first music as a species, their call notes the first living patterns on our collective human eardrum. We learned percussion from the woodpecker and to scream from the eagle and to sing complicated melody from the warbler and the thrush.

Just as our bodies are constructed of the dust of stars, they also carry the memory of a time when our lives were always with the birds, out under the spread of the sky. A time when we lived without separation.

Bill McKibben, perhaps the most effective and tireless advocate in the United States on the issue of climate change, says this: "How do you cope with celebrating a dying world when you think you should be trying to save it? You—we—are required to bear witness to it. This is one of our jobs. It's as close to religious duty as one could imagine." We must keep watch over these beautiful lives and pray for directions to inform our actions on their behalf and our own.

How is the dementia we are inflicting on our world similar to a dementing illness in a single human brain? It is this: in both cases, the afflicted suffer from the paradigm of perpetual growth, the smothering and overexploitation of diversely beautiful and unprotected, common resources. In human dementia, the losses are painfully observable. One by one the life forces are dissolved. Dancing, laughing, smiling, problem solving, remembering and imagining, and eventually breathing are all stolen from the individual.

For the Earth, the dementing disease—our system of economic and political dominance—has terminated the Cenozoic era, the time of this planet's maximum flowering and biodiversity, and replaced it with the largest extinction event in sixty-five million years. One million species have been already lost and replaced with a spiraling increase in human biomass. Industrial civilization has induced an apparently unstoppable climate crisis of epic proportions.

In his last years, we did for our father everything we could, with the full and gathering knowledge of the eventual outcome. We knew he would die and he did. Is our Earth also terminally ill? Does the human-induced pace of species extinction and climate crisis ensure that we will also lose our Mother?

I believe that we can redeem our species. As Amitav Ghosh has written, the derangement of our times is rooted in how we live. That's the difference between my father's illness and the illness of the Earth: the latter is animated by cumulative human actions, guided by legal and economic systems that treat the natural world as property to be exploited, not as an ecological partner. It follows that we can mitigate, to some extent, the wounding of our planet's climate and biodiversity. Transforming our culture, our assumptions, our worldview, our cosmology of separation, our economies—that is the single bird we must heal.

But the work has to start now, and it has to be swift. The systems of power that have done the damage will not lead, nor should they be allowed. We're on our own, but we are billions.

Acknowledgments

My uncle Don Isleib walked the journey with his brother every single day. Those two men shared a lifetime companionship, and from their example, many of us have forged our own. Uncle Don, we love you so.

I honor my siblings, who shared the love and lives of our father and mother: Roberta Isleib, Doug Isleib, and Martha Taylor. There wasn't a day when my sister Bobbie failed to call and consult and console and support Dad and me. My brother-in-law John Brady grounded us. Our cousins and grandchildren understand the privilege of being born into this lineage. I am grateful for all my human relations, especially Elise Smith, Hannah and Asa Canter, Erin Canter, Rachel Williams, and Casey and Patrick Chanton.

I honor the work of all the caregivers who eased my father's last years. Faithfulness is their true name, but they also go by Esmine McCormick, Jill Welch, Gail Daly, Shirley M., and Beulah A. An army of women and men dedicate their lives to the care of our elders, and we owe them far better pay and working conditions than they currently receive.

Dr. Ken Brummel-Smith is a guiding force in the field of aging and death with dignity. We leaned on his honesty and strength, as have so many others.

I believe I remember every single kindness extended to us during the years we cared for Dad. Special gratitude to Norine Cardea, Ann Morrow, Velma Frye, Julie Morris, Crystal Wakoa, David Moynahan, Rebecca Clemens, Martha Paradeis, Barry Fraser, Lucy Ann Walker-Fraser, Gretchen Hein, Tom and Margaret Clark, Donna Klein, Terry Schneider, the Grambor family, and my Womenspirit sisters.

I thank my first readers and my writing companions. For believing in my pages: Roberta Isleib, Mary Jane Ryals, Kathleen Laufenberg, Donna Decker, Wilderness Sarchild, and Amrita Brummel-Smith. Thank you, Eileen Albrigo. The counsel and love of Janisse Ray is essential to my writing and advocacy work in the world. Deena Metzger is more important to me than I can say. Lou Cross, I still miss our long creative partnership.

Our family is grateful to the staff of Big Bend Hospice—music therapists, social workers, clergy, and nurses—for their personal attention. We were so lucky to partake of their services in those years. The Reverend Candace McKibben is the kindest, most generous person I know, and she released Dad from this world spiritually, in his last hours.

It was a great gift to bury my father at the Prairie Creek Conservation Cemetery near Gainesville, Florida, where sandhill cranes stalk and swallow-tailed kites soar, a place that considers land and resources and reunites people with the Earth. Freddie Johnson was our compassionate guide.

I am so very grateful (all of us should be) for those who spend their lives stewarding the wild birds and places on this burning, besieged planet. Too many to name, every single one a hero. We must all join their ranks fighting climate change and stemming biodiversity losses.

James Patrick Allen, Jon Davies, and all the staff at the University of Georgia Press make so many important, beautiful books, year after year after year. I know how lucky I am to birth yet another volume with them. May we continue.

Thank you to my beloved son, David. I honor your courage, your honesty, your persistence, your love, and how you brought Hannah and Asa into our lives. You said: "Mom, I think you are writing this book to stay connected to Grandpa." You were right.

Jeff, thank you for walking the path of life with me so well and truly. I am so grateful for our partnership.